A TEXT BOOK OF

ICSE
COMPUTER
APPLICATIONS

In accordance with the latest syllabus prescribed by the Council for the Indian Certificate of Secondary Education, New Delhi.

A TEXT BOOK OF

ICSE

COMPUTER APPLICATIONS

CLASS IX

By

Rupa Pandit

MCA, Head of Dept. (Computer Science)

The Assembly of God Church School (Kolkata)

OSWAL PUBLISHERS

1/12, Sahitya Kunj, M. G. Road, Agra-282 002

Edition : 2019

OSWAL PUBLISHERS

Head office	: 1/12, Sahitya Kunj, M.G. Road, Agra-282 002
Phone	: (0562) 2527771- 4, + 91 75340 77222
E-mail	: contact@oswalpublishers.com, sales@oswalpublishers.com
Website	: www.oswalpublishers.com
Facebook link	: https://www.facebook.com/oswalpublishersindia
Available at	: amazon.in, Flipkart, snapdeal, paytm
Printed at	: Upkar Printing Unit, Agra

Preface

We are privileged to present the new edition of ICSE Computer Applications text book for class IX. This book aims at providing the relevant content as per the latest guidelines prescribed by the Council for the Indian Certificate of Secondary Education Examination, New Delhi. The book covers all the topics in accordance with the latest syllabus in a simple, lucid and detailed manner. The purpose behind writing this book is to develop the ability of the students to understand the curriculum of computers in an interesting way.

Silent Features of this book includes :

- The topics are covered from initial fundamentals in each chapter.
- Plenty of solved exercises and programs with algorithmic detail.
- A variety of supporting examples for clarification of each topic.
- Brief and detailed explanations for the better understanding of every concept.
- Point wise description of all the topics.
- The REMEMBER BOX to sharpen the memory of the students.
- Solved previous examination questions in each chapter.
- Model papers are included at the end of this book.

Special care has been taken to explain those topics in detail where students often get confused. Efforts have been put to solve the actual doubts faced by the students that are encountered while learning.

We hope this new edition will be welcomed by all with warmth and generosity and would find this book useful.

The author would like to thank the Almighty for His grace and blessings, gratitude expressed to family, friends and each student for their love and continuous support.

Inspite of our best efforts, the possibilities of some errors of omission and commission cannot be ruled out. Constructive suggestions will be appreciated and thankfully acknowledged. Please feel free to mail your opinion and queries at oswalpublishers@ gmail.com.

—PUBLISHER

SYLLABUS CLASS IX
COMPUTER APPLICATIONS (86)

Aims :

1. *To empower students by enabling them to build their own applications.*

2. *To introduce students to some effective tools to enable them to enhance their knowledge, broaden horizons, foster creativity, improve the quality of work and increase efficiency.*

3. *To develop logical and analytical thinking so that they can easily solve interactive programs.*

4. *To help students learn fundamental concepts of computing using object oriented approach in one computer language.*

5. *To provide students with a clear idea of ethical issues involved in the field of computing.*

There will be one written paper of two hours duration carrying 100 marks and Internal Assessment of 100 marks.

The paper will be divided into two sections A and B.

Section A (Compulsory – 40 marks) will consist of compulsory short answer questions covering the entire syllabus.

Section B (60 marks) will consist of questions which will require detailed answers. There will be a choice of questions in this section.

PART I - THEORY 100 Marks

1. Introduction to Object Oriented Programming concepts

    (i) Principles of Object Oriented Programming, (Difference between Procedure Oriented and Object oriented).

    All the four principles of Object Oriented programming should be defined and explained using real life examples (Data abstraction, Inheritance, Polymorphism, Encapsulation).

    (ii) Introduction to JAVA-Types of java programs—Applets and Applications, Java Compilation process, Java Source code, Byte code, Object code, Java Virtual Machine (JVM), Features of JAVA.

    Definition of Java applets and Java applications with examples, steps involved in compilation process, definitions of source code, byte code, object code, JVM, features of JAVA-Simple, Robust, secured, object oriented, platform independent, etc.

2. Elementary concept of Objects and Classes

    Modelling entities and their behaviour by objects, a class as a specification for objects and as an object factory, computation as message passing/ method calls between objects (many examples should be done to illustrate this). Objects encapsulate state (attributes) and have behaviour (methods). Class as a user defined data type.

    A class may be regarded as a blueprint to create objects. It may be viewed as a factory that produces similar objects. A class may also be considered as a new data type created by the user, that has its own functionality.

3. Values and data types

    Character set, ASCII code, Unicode, Escape sequences, Tokens, Constants and Variables, Data types, type conversions.

    Escape sequences [\n, \t, \\, \", \'], Tokens and its types [keywords, identifiers, literals, punctuators, operators], Primitive types and non-primitive types with examples,

Introduce the primitive types with size in bits and bytes, Implicit type conversion and Explicit type conversions.

4. Operators in Java

Forms of operators, Types of operators, Counters, Accumulators, Hierarchy of operators, 'new' operator, dot (.) operator.

Forms of operators (Unary, Binary, Ternary), types of operators (Arithmetic, Relational, Logical, Assignment, Increment, Decrement, Short hand operators), Discuss precedence and associativity of operators, prefix and postfix, Creation of dynamic memory by using new operator, invoking members of class using dot operator, Introduce System.out.prinln() and System.out.print()-for simple output.

(Bitwise and shift operators are not included.)

5. Input in Java

Initialization, Parameter, introduction to packages, Input streams (Scanner Class), types of errors, types of comments.

Initialization—Data before execution, Parameters—at the time of execution, input stream-data entry during execution-using methods of Scanner class [nextShort(), nextInt(), nextLong(), nextDouble(), next(), nextLine(), next(). charAt(0)].

Discuss different types of errors occurring during execution and compilation of the program (syntax errors, runtime errors and logical errors). Singe line comment (//) and multiline comment (/*....*/)

6. Mathematical Library Methods

Introduction to package java.lang [default], methods of Math class.

pow(x,y), sqrt(x), cbrt(x), ceil(x), floor(x), round(x), abs(a), max(a, b), min(a,b), random().

Java expressions—using all the operators and methods of Math class.

7. Conditional constructs in Java

Application of if, if else, if else if ladder, switch-case, default, break.

if, if else, if else if, Nested if, switch case, break statement, fall through condition in switch case, Menu driven programs, System.exit(0)-to terminate the program.

8. Iterative constructs in Java

Definition, Types of looping statements, entry controlled loops [for, while], exit controlled loop [do while], variations in looping statements, and Jump statements.

Syntax of entry and exit controlled loops, break and continue, Simple programs illustrating all three loops, inter conversion from for—while—do while, finite and infinite, delay, multiple counter variables (initializations and updations). Demonstrate break and continue statements with the help of loops.

Loops are fundamenta to computation and their need should be shown by examples.

9. Nested for loops

Introduce nested loops through some simple examples. Demonstrate break and continue statements with the help of nested loops.

Programs based on nested loops [rectangular, triangular [right angled triangle only] patterns], series involving single variable.

(Nested while and nested do while are not included).

10. Computing and Ethics

Ethical Issues in Computing.

PART II - INTERNAL ASSESSMENT

100 Marks

This segment of the syllabus is totally practical oriented. The accent is on acquiring basic programming skills quickly and efficiently.

Programming Assignments (Class IX)

Students are expected to do a minimum of 20 assignments during the whole year to reinforce the concepts studied in the class.

Suggested list of Assignments :

The laboratory assignments will form the bulk of the course. Good assignments should have problems which require design, implementation and testing. They should also embody one or more concepts that have been discussed in the theory class. A significant proportion of the time has to be spent in the laboratory. Computing can only be learnt by doing.

The teacher-in-charge should maintain a record of all the assignments done as a part of practical work throughout the year and give it due credit at he time of cumulative evaluation at the end of the year.

Some sample problems are given below as examples. The problems are of varying levels of difficulty :

(i) Programs using Assignment statements.

Example : Calculation of Area/Volume/Conversion of temperature/Swapping of values etc.

(ii) Programs based on-Input through parameters.

Example : Implementation of standard formula etc.

(iii) Programs based on-Input through Scanner class.

Example : Implementation of standard formula etc.

(iv) Programs based on Mathematical methods.

Example : larger/smaller of two numbers, cube root, square root, absolute value, power, etc.

(v) Programs based on if, if else, if else if ladder, nested if etc.

    (a) if programs

- Larger/smaller of two numbers
- To check divisibility of a number, etc.

    (b) if else programs

- Odd or even number
- Eligibility to vote
- Upper case or lower case
- Positive or negative number
- Vowel or Consonant
- Buzz number etc.

    (c) if-else-if programs

- Programs based on discount/interest/bonus/taxes/commission.
- Programs based on slab system.
- Programs based on Nested if.

(vi) Programs on switch case.

    (a) Day of a week

    (b) Name of the month

(c) Names of the seasons

(d) Calculator

(e) Vowel or consonant etc.

(vii) Programs based on Looping Statement

    (a) Programs based on for looping statement

    (b) Programs based on printing simple series, summation of simple series, product of simple series.

    (c) Prime number, perfect number, composite number, Fibonacci series. Lowest Common Multiple (LCM), Highest Common Factor (HCF) etc.

    (d) To find the biggest and smallest number from n number of entered numbers

    (e) Program based on while loop like Armstrong number, Spy number, Niven number, Palindrome number, etc.

(viii) Programs based on nested loops [rectangular, triangular (right angled triangle only) patterns], series involving single variable.

(ix) Generate first n multiples of numbers from 1 to the limit input by the user.

(x) Menu Driven programs.

Important : This list is indicative only. Teachers and student should use their imagination to create innovative and original assignments.

EVALUATION

Proposed Guidelines for Marking

The teacher should use the criteria below to judge the internal work done. Basically, four criteria are being suggested: class design, coding and documentation, variable description and execution or output. The acutal grading will be done by the teacher based on his/her judgment. However, one possible way: divide the outcome for each criterion into one of 4 groups : excellent, good, fair/acceptable, poor/ unacceptable, then use numeric values for each grade and add to get the total.

Class design

Has a suitable class (or classes) been used ?

Are all attributes with the right kinds of types present ?

Is encapsulation properly done ?

Is the interface properly designed ?

Coding and Documentation

Is the coding done properly? (choice of names, no unconditional jumps, proper organization of conditions, proper choice of loops, error handling code layout). Is the documentation complete and readable ? (class documentation, variable documentation, method documentation, constraints, known bugs-if any).

Variable and Description

Format for variable description :

Name of the variable	Data Type	Purpose/Description

Subject teacher (Internal Examiner):   100 marks

Criteria (Total-100 marks	Class design (20 marks)	Variable description (20 marks)	Coding and Documentation (20 marks)	Execution OR Output (40 marks)
Excellent	20	20	20	40
Good	16	16	16	32
Fair	12	12	12	12
Poor	8	8	8	16

CONTENTS

OBJECT ORIENTED PROGRAMMING CONCEPTS

Contents
- Introduction
- Object-Oriented Programming (OOP)
  - ❖ Four Main principles of OOP Programming
  - ❖ OOP vs. Procedure Oriented Programming
- Object
- Class
  - ❖ Class is an object factory
  - ❖ Class as a user-defined data type
- Abstraction
- Encapsulation
  - ❖ Object encapsulates state & behavior
- Inheritance
- Polymorphism
- Message Passing
- Summary
- Solved Questions
- Exercise

INTRODUCTION

Object-Oriented Programming is a model of programming languages, based on creating partitioned memory area for both data and methods. OOP, as it is also known, is a modern approach to programming that overcomes various shortcomings associated with procedural programming languages.

Procedural programming languages are based on breaking up a program into a number of functions. **Functions are the key element in procedural programming languages** and there will be an associative function for each specific task that the system needs to perform. The communication between the systems takes place by passing data between these functions.

This is why, **Procedural Programming languages are also known as Functions Oriented Programming languages.**

Object-Oriented Programming, on the other hand, is analogous to the real world. A program in Object-Oriented Programming is composed of real world entities called objects. **Objects represent the key element of OOP's** and their behavior are specified by defining methods. The communication between objects takes place via methods just like people communicate by requesting information in the real world scenario.

This is why **Object-Oriented Programming languages are also known as Data-Oriented Programming languages.**

OBJECT-ORIENTED PROGRAMMING (OOP)

It is a kind of programming language in which classes generate objects and define their structure, like a blueprint and the objects are created to implement the tasks as intended by the computer program by interacting among each other. Java, C++ are some examples of OOP languages.

Four Main Principles of OOP Programming

- **Encapsulation :** It means all data and methods are enclosed in a class.
- **Inheritance :** It is a feature in which a derived (child) class is being able to access data/methods of its base (parent) class. This feature helps in code reusability.
- **Polymorphism :** It is an ability of methods to have same name but to behave differently under different situations.
- **Abstraction :** It is an ability to apply the method without knowing the method details.

OOP Vs. Procedure Oriented Programming

OOP	POP
Follows bottom-up approach	Follows top-down approach
Supports inheritance, encapsulation, abstraction, polymorphism, etc	Supports Modular Programming
Programs are divided into small entities called objects	Programs are divided into small self-contained functions
More secure as having data hiding feature	Less secure as there is no way of data hiding
Provides more reusability, less function dependency	Provides less reusability, more function dependency
More abstraction and more flexibility	Less abstraction and less flexibility
Overloading is possible in the form of function and operator overloading	Overloading is not possible of any type
Has access specifiers named Public, Private, Protected, etc	POP does not have any access specifier. All the members are public

OOP provides an easy way to add new data and functions	To add new data and function in POP is not so easy
Examples of OOP are C++, JAVA, VB.NET, C#.NET	Examples of POP are C, VB, FORTRAN, Pascal

OBJECT

An **object** is an instance of a class. The object brings a class to the real world.

Definition : An Object can be considered as an entity that has a specific identity, characteristics and behavior.

An object in the real world can be one of the following :

- Anything that may be apprehended intellectually.
- To which a thought or action is directed.
- Anything that is visible or tangible.

If anything in the world meets the above criteria, you can say that it is an object. It exhibits unique behavior, characteristics and also has a unique identity.

CLASS

A **class** is a blueprint to create objects. In other words, we can say that a class provides a definition for an item/object. It provides the data and methods[1] (functions) that all objects have.

A class refers to a group of similar kind of objects. Before understanding the meaning of a class, recall the definition of an object. An object is something that possesses state and behaviour. Here, the objects which possess similar state and behavior are grouped to form a class. For example, consider two different types of fan.

State	Fan1	Fan2
Color	Black	Brown
No of wings	3	4
Brand	Khaitan	PSPO
Behavior	FAN 1	FAN 2
	ON	ON
	OFF	OFF

You can see that the two specified fans have the same state or features although, they have different values for them. They also exhibit similar behavior (On and Off). Now, we can combine these two fans to form a class of fans with many other variants of a fan. So here, **Fan** represents a class of fans whereas, **Fan1** and **Fan2** are the objects of the class **Fan**.

Let us look into some examples from the real world to understand Classes and Objects.

[only few members of the class are given here]

---

1. A method contains program code which when executed performs certain task. A method can also be called a process or a function.

- Class Name – Bottle

  Member Data – capacity, color, brand name, item_contained

  Member Methods – get_filled, get_dried

  (All bottles around us are the objects of class Bottle)

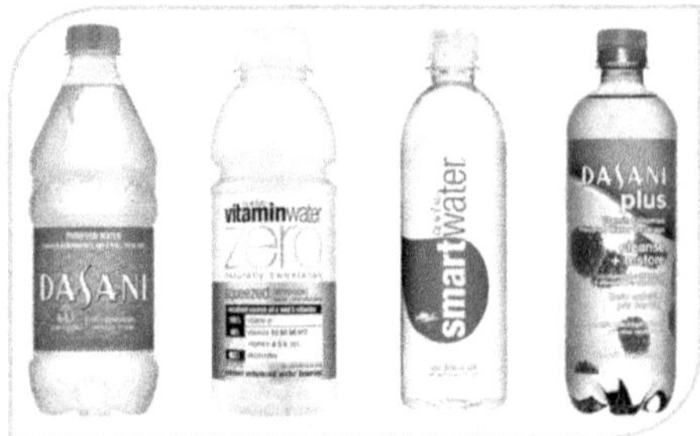

Fig. 1.1

- Class Name – Bank

  Member Data – name, total_customers, total_employees and revenue_stored

  Member Methods – deposit, withdrawal and open_account

  (Different banks are the objects of class Bank)

Fig. 1.2

- Class Name – School

  Member Data – name, board_name, total_students, total_staff and founding_year

  Member Methods – admission, attendance, examination and sports

  (different schools are the objects of the Class School)

Fig. 1.3

Thus, we can say that objects are instances of a class. A class is an object factory from where many objects can be created.

Class is an object factory

A class is said to be the producer of objects. The class takes information about how to create objects, which may be in the form of values of an object's state and its behavior and the value returned is the actual created object or its reference (its instance).

In simpler terms, a class is an **object factory or object maker.** As it stores all the information that is required to create the objects and their features. It also groups the operations that can be performed by the object.

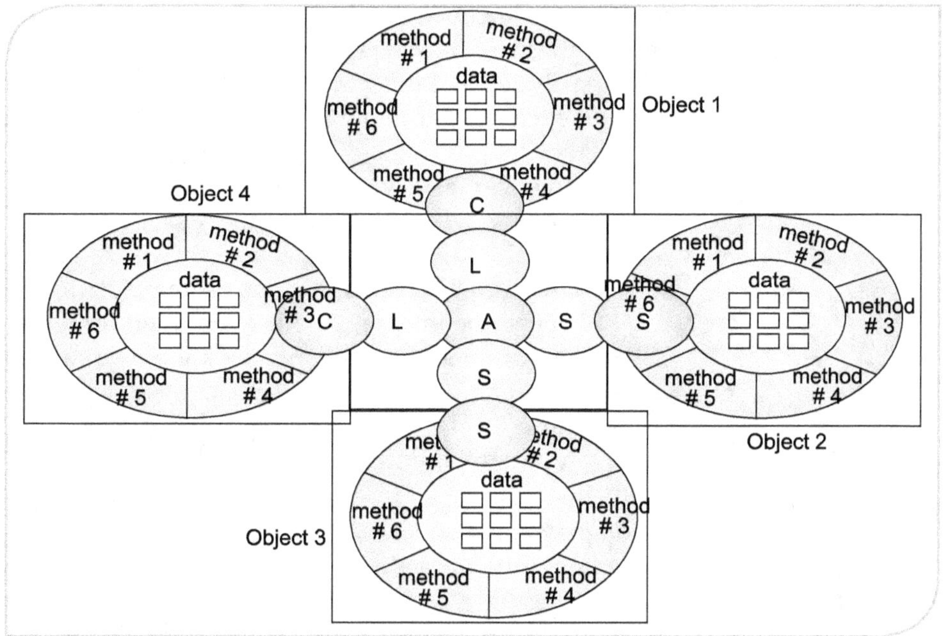

Fig. 1.4 : Class as a factory of objects

Class as a User-Defined Data Type

User-defined data type means that the user creates what he/she needs as per his/ her requirement or choice. If we look around us, there are many user-defined objects which are made using elementary objects. For example, consider a cupboard as a user-defined data type which is made up of elementary objects such as wood, glass, nobs, etc.

User-defined type of data allows a user to create composite data of his/her choice. It may include variety of primitive data types[2] as well as other composite data types[3] and also a set of methods or functions. Object-oriented programming permits the creation of user-defined data as per his/her requirement. This gives flexibility to a program and allows the user to create a versatile program. User-defined data type also comes with an option of having methods that can be used for initialization and modification of member data.

ABSTRACTION

It is a concept which gives stress on the ability to apply a method without knowing the details of it. It is a way of representing a real world situation in its most important elements. The concept of abstraction can be explained with the help of the following example:

---

2. Primitive data types are readily available for programmer's use. Java has eight primitive data types, which are boolean, char, byte, short, int, long, float and double. Example: int v = 5; double d = 2.9;
3. Composite data types are generally made up of multiple primitive data types. They are created by the programmer in a program and they can vary in their structure from program to program. Java provides two composite data types – classes and arrays. Example of composite data type - class Student {String name; int age; double marks;}

Suppose you want to switch on your fan. All you need to do is that press the ON button for the fan and it will start running. You can easily see that the fan starts running as soon as you switch the fan to the ON position.

Any representation of data in which the implementation details are hidden is known as data abstraction.

However, have you ever wondered why the fan starts running when you press the ON button? Did you ever think of the internal process which sets the fan running? What happens inside the electrical circuits ? Here, the internal details are hidden from the users. This hidden functionality is known as abstraction.

Fig. 1.5

Abstraction shows only the important things while hiding the background functionality.

Other examples are, a person may know how to use a mobile phone but may not know the intricate details of how it is made.

Similarly, a person may know how to drive a car but may not know how to repair it.

Fig. 1.6

ENCAPSULATION

Encapsulation refers to the binding of features and behavior of an object in a single unit. In simple words, it is a concept in which all data and methods are enclosed in a class.

In other words, we can say that encapsulation is a concept that helps to gather all important and relevant requirements within one boundary.

Lets consider 'Hospital' as a class. The word creates an impression in mind that there are many components that are included in a single unit of Hospital. The components can be considered as cardiac unit, ENT unit, pharmacy unit, neurologic unit, pathology unit, canteen, account unit, etc. Hence, we can say, a Hospital encapsulates all the important and relevant units within one boundary.

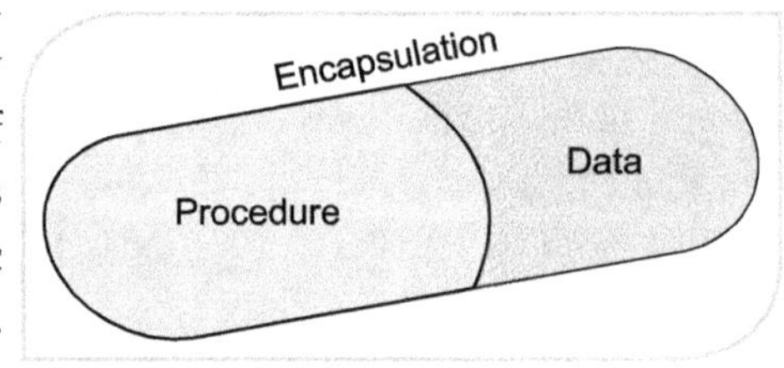

Fig. 1.7

Let us take another example, 'School' as a class. The concept of encapsulation brings together all the relevant data such as school name, board_name, total_students, total_staff, founding_year and procedures such as admission, attendance, examination, sports, etc.

Thus, we can say that encapsulation refers to keeping data and the behavior of the data in one capsule known as a class.

Object Encapsulates State & Behavior

According to Grady Booch, a renowned software architect, an object has the following characteristics:

1. It has a state.
2. It may display behavior.
3. It has a unique identity.

The state of an object is indicated by a set of attributes and their values. Specifically, the state of an object refers to the particular set of values of the data members. As time passes, the state of an object can change, i.e. one or more values of the data members can change.

As we have discussed *state*, let us now understand what behavior is? We normally associate the word with (a) the way an object acts through time, (b) the way an object reacts to its environment (the input), (c) the actions that depend upon its current state. This is what behavior means. Behavior is the way, in which the object responds to a particular stimulus, in a particular state and at a particular time.

As we know, objects are instances of a class and they implement all that is within a class. When a class encapsulates the relevant data and methods, the objects implement them in the real world. This makes objects encapsulate states and behaviors of the class they belongs to.

For example, consider a class 'Zebra' having four objects. All the objects of Zebra would have the states of class Zebra such as age, height, weight, etc and behavior such as eating, sleeping, running, etc.

INHERITANCE

It is a concept in which a class gets access to the members of another class. Inheritance is a major component of object-oriented programming. Inheritance refers to the process of creating new classes, called derived classes from existing classes or base classes. The derived class

> **REMEMBER**
> *The class getting access to another class is called the derived class.*

inherits all the capabilities of the base class but can also add features of its own too. Many of the objects in the real world have common features.

Inheritance facilitates code reusability. The same code need not be written repeatedly incase multiple usages are needed. With the help of inheritance, the more frequently required code can be made the super/ base class and it can be inherited by other classes who would like to use the methods given by it.

> **REMEMBER**
> *The class giving access to another class is called the base class.*

Secondly, in our real life, we can see examples of Inheritance in many forms. When a parent allows his/her child to access his/her products, then the concept of inheritance gets illustrated.

For example, let the base class be 'Shape'. It can have three derived classes, Rectangle, Triangle and Circle. These derived classes can inherit features from their base class.

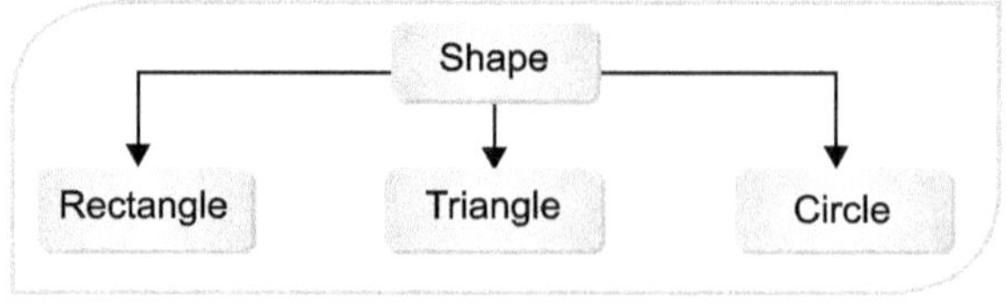

Fig. 1.8

POLYMORPHISM

Polymorphism refers to the ability to exist in more than one form. In object-oriented programming, polymorphism refers to the implementation of objects in different ways based on their classes or data types. It is a concept in which the same methods behave differently under different situations. The arguments of the method decide the course of action to be taken by the program.

Interestingly, the word polymorphism is derived from two words, Poly and Morphism. The meaning of poly is multiple and morphism is forms. It makes the meaning of polymorphism as Multiple Forms.

For example, the process of heating makes different objects behave differently. Water when heated, gets evaporated. Ice when heated, gets melted. Paper when heated, gets burnt. In this way, we see that the same operation heating makes three objects behave differently.

For example, the same person can be a student in school, a player in the playground and an artist in a drawing class.

Fig. 1.9

MESSAGE PASSING

By now we have seen that a class is a blueprint and an object is an instance of a class. There can be multiple objects of a class.

Once objects come into existence, they start functioning. When multiple objects are functioning, there arises a need for communication between them. The communication between objects of a class is called **message passing**. Message passing is applied when the result of some operation of one object is required by another operation of another object.

Message passing is done using methods or functions. Message passing is also known as **inter-process communication**.

Consider an example of a **student** as an object. When there are multiple student objects, one student object can send a message to another student object about the basketball tournament to be conducted in the evening in the local basketball court.

Consider another example of **passport** as an object. One process may ask for information about the validity of visa status to another process. Message interaction taking place between processes is called **inter-process communication**. It plays an important role in message passing.

Fig. 1.10

SUMMARY

- A **class** is a blueprint to create objects.
- An **object** is an instance of a class. The object brings a class to the real world.
- A class is an object factory from where many objects can be created.
- **Main Principles** of OOP Language: Encapsulation, Inheritance, Polymorphism and Abstraction
- **Encapsulation :** It means all data and methods are enclosed in a class.
- **Inheritance :** It is a feature in which a derived (child) class is being able to access data/methods of its base (parent) class. This feature helps in code reusability.
- **Polymorphism :** It is an ability of methods to have same name but to behave differently under different situations.
- **Abstraction :** It is an ability to apply the method without knowing the method details.
- A class is said to be the producer of objects.
- User defined data type means that the user creates what he/she needs as per requirement or choice.
- The communication between the objects of a class is called **message passing**.
- Message interaction taking place between processes is called **inter-process communication**.

SOLVED QUESTIONS

1. **What is a class and an object ?**

   Answer : A **class** is a blueprint to create objects. In other words, we can say that a class provides a definition for an item/object. It provides the data and methods (functions) that all the objects have.

   An object is an instance of a class. The object brings a class to the real world. An object can be considered as an entity that has a specific identity, characteristics and behavior.

2. **How we can say that a class is an object factory ?**

   Answer : A class is said to be the producer of objects. A class takes information about how to create objects, which may be in the form of values of an object's state and behaviour and the value returned is the actual created object or its reference (its instance). Thus, a class is an object factory.

3. **Explain Inheritance and also define base class and derived class :**

   Answer : It is a concept in which a class gets access to the members of another class. Inheritance is a major component of object-oriented programming. Inheritance refers to the process of creating new classes called derived classes from existing classes or base classes. The derived class inherits all the capabilities of the base class but can also add features of its own too. Many of the objects in the real world have common features.

   Inheritance facilitates code reusability. The same code need not be written repeatedly incase multiple usage is needed. With the help of inheritance, the more frequently required code can be made the super/base class and it can be inherited by other classes who would like to use the methods given by it.

   The class giving access to another class is called the base class.

   The class getting access to another class is called the derived class

4. **Explain object encapsulates state & behavior.**

   Answer : Objects are instances of a class and they implement all that is within a class. When a class encapsulates the relevant data and methods, the objects implement them in the real world. This makes objects encapsulate states and behaviors of the class they belong to.

   For example, consider a class 'Zebra' having 4 objects. All the objects of Zebra would have the states of class Zebra such as age, height, weight, etc and behavior such as eating, sleeping, running, etc.

5. **Define Polymorphism with example.**

   Answer : Polymorphism refers to the ability to exist in more than one form. In Object-Oriented Programming, Polymorphism refers to the implementation of objects in different ways based on their classes or data types. It is a concept in which the same method behaves differently under different situations. The arguments of the method decide the course of action to be taken by the program.

6. **Name the features of Object-Oriented Programming.**

   Answer : Features of OOP Language: Encapsulation, Inheritance, Polymorphism and Abstraction.

7. **Abstraction and Encapsulation are complementary concepts ? Explain how ?**

   Answer : Abstraction shows only the important things while hiding the background functionality.

   Encapsulation, on the other hand, is a concept in which all the data and methods are enclosed in a class.

   Thus, abstraction speaks about hiding the background details whereas encapsulation speaks about enclosing all the member data and methods to be presented in a class. Hence, they are complementary concepts.

EXERCISE

Question 1. Answer the following :

  (a) How is a class and an object related to each other ?

  (b) What is Object-Oriented Programming (OOP) ?

  (c) Write the main features of OOP language ?

  (d) What is the difference between 'Encapsulation' and 'Abstraction' ?

  (e) What is message passing ?

  (f) Give two examples of real world objects. Also specify their characteristics and behaviour.

  (g) State the differences between object-oriented programming and procedural-oriented programming.

Question 2. Given the following situations, identify the objects of the class :

  (a) In a car showroom, there were many cars.

  (b) All the students in the class were chatting.

  (c) None of the pens in the pencil box had red ink.

  (d) I got all new 100 rupee notes from the bank.

  (e) The librarian was busy restoring the torn books of the library.

  (f) After watching the movie, the audience was spellbound.

  (g) All the guests were given a flower bouquet each.

  (h) The passengers, going to Delhi, carried food with them.

  (i) In the computer lab, all the computers had LCD monitors.

  (j) The company offered a flat discount of 20% on a range of wrist watches.

Question 3. Given the following situations, identify the Object-Oriented Programming concept [Encapsulation, Abstraction, Polymorphism and Inheritance :

  (a) Inside the fort, all the facilities were present.

  (b) Ruma did not know why her computer was not getting started so she could not work on her project report in Word.

  (c) Did you know that the famous painter Ritoja was also a good dancer ?

  (d) The noble teacher allowed his students to share his books and notes.

  (e) Code developers give only the executable file for users. So the users do not know the code details but can use the application programs.

INTRODUCTION TO JAVA– DATA VALUES AND TYPES

Contents

INTRODUCTION

Java is a programming language that has many features. Java has been developed by a team led by James Gosling. The language was initially called 'Oak', after an oak tree that stood outside Gosling's office. It was later renamed as 'Java', after Java coffee. Java is based on object oriented concept. Debugging and compiling is easy in Java so it allows us to develop many applications. Java became a popular language for Internet because of its features.

Brief History of Java

In 1995, Java was first launched by Sun Microsystems. The team started working in 1991 as "Green Team", whose aim was to unite digital consumer devices and computers and they invented a new language. The new language that they developed was equipped with an interactive, handheld home entertainment controller that was originally targeted at the digital cable television industry. Unfortunately, the concept was too advanced for the team at that time. But the technology was just right for the Internet, which was just starting to take off. In 1995, the team announced that the Netscape Navigator Internet browser would incorporate Java technology.

Java has been through many development phases and gone through regular upgrading. On November 13 of 2006, Sun released much of its **java virtual machines** (JVM) as **"free and open sources software"** (FOSS), under the term of GNU **General Public Licence** (GPL). The making of JVM core code was finished on 8th May 2007 and made available as free/open-source software. In 2010, Oracle acquired Sun Microsystems. The latest version of Java is Version-8 that has come out in 2014 and last updated in March 2017.

Today, Java not only permeates the Internet, but also is the invisible force behind many applications and devices that power our day-to-day lives. From mobile phones to handheld devices, games and navigation systems to e-business solutions, Java is everywhere.

Features of Java

I.   Platform Independent : Programs written in Java can be executed on any other platform (such as Windows, Unix, Linux, Mac OS, etc) that has the Java virtual machine (JVM).

II. Portable : The feature of Platform Independence makes a Java program portable and follows the concept "Write Once Run Anywhere (WORA)".

III. Object-Oriented : Java is an OOPL that supports the construction of programs that consist of collections of collaborating objects. These objects have a unique identity, encapsulate attributes and operations, and are instances of classes related by inheritance and polymorphism.

IV. Simple : Java was designed with a small number of language constructs so that programmers could learn it quickly. It eliminates several language features available in C/C++ that are associated with poor programming practices or are rarely used.

V. Secure : Java is designed to be secure in a networked environment. The Java run-time environment uses a bytecode verification process to ensure that the code loaded over the network does not violate Java security constraints.

VI. Robust : Java is designed to eliminate certain types of programming errors. Java is strongly typed, which allows extensive compile-time error checking. It does not support memory pointers, which eliminates the possibility of overwriting memory and corrupting data. In addition, its automatic memory management (garbage collection) eliminates memory leaks and other problems associated with dynamic memory allocation/de-allocation.

VII. Wide Application Area : Java programming language can be used in developing programs of various kinds. It is also used in a variety of devices for implementing solutions such as networking of PCs, the Internet, mobile and entertainment software, etc.

Java Applets & Application

Have you ever wondered how videos or animation work on a website? Java applets help make the magic happen. You might think that web page coding such as HTML is naturally interactive. But HTML and other markup language are static. Java applets are small pieces of code that work in another program. They help make a page more dynamic.

A Java Applet is a small and efficient Java program, which is used for internet programming. Applets are typically executed in an AppletViewer, but they can also be executed in HTML[1]. The applet is usually embedded in an HTML page on a Web site and can be executed from within a browser.

```
/*
A Java Applet Example
*/
import java.applet.Applet;
import java.awt.Graphics;
/*
<applet code = "AppletEg" width = 150 height = 175>
</applet>
*/
public class AppletEg extends Applet
{
    public void paint(Graphics g)
    {
        //a simple instruction
        g.drawString("Helow. Welcome to Java Applets", 20, 100);
    }
}
```

---

1. HTML is used to create electronic documents (called web pages) that are displayed on the World Wide Web. Each page contains a series of connectioons to other pages called hyperlinks. Every web page you see on the Internet is written using one version of HTML code or another.

Java Application is a Java program that has an aim and can be executed as a single program. It does not require any browser. The program gets converted to executable code by the JVM or the Java Virtual Machine.

Java Source Code

Java Source Code is the program written by a programmer in Java language. It is written by the programmer by using the instructions specified for achieving a purpose.

Compilation Process

A Java program, when compiled by the Java compiler, creates the Java Byte Code for that program.

Compiler byte code is the result of the compilation of a Java program, an intermediate representation of that program which is machine independent. The Java bytecode gets processed by the Java virtual machine (JVM) instead of the processor.

Java Bytecode

Java code is compiled to create Java Bytecode which is processed by Java virtual machine. This code is independent of the processor of the computer system. The portability or machine independence of a Java program is because of this Java Bytecode.

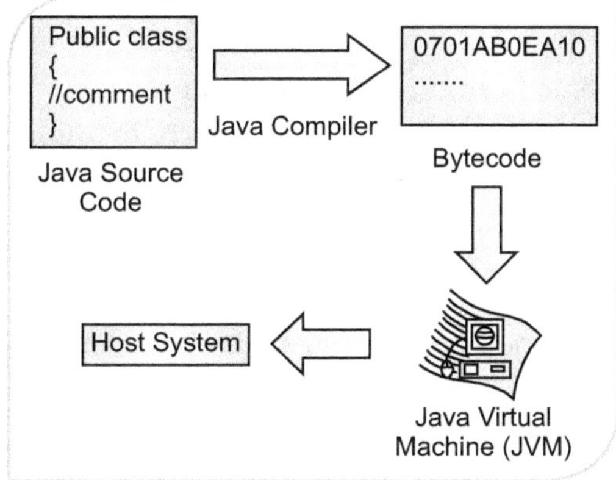

Fig. 2.1

Object Code

The feature of portability of Java language requires a Java program to get converted to an object code during compilation. This object code is closest to machine code and the Java compiler generates the corresponding machine language code.

Java Virtual Machine (JVM)

This is a software that converts Java Bytecode to machine language. It works as a platform for a Java program, and can be executed on any platform (Windows, Unix,

Linux, etc). JVM comes in between a compiled Java code and computer system. JVM is the main component of the Java architecture and is a part of Java runtime environment (JRE)[2]. JVM combined with Java API (Application Program Interface) makes the Java Platform.

Most compilers provide code for a computer system but Java compiler produces code for JVM. This provides security and portability to a Java program.

Java Program → [Java Compiler] → **Java Bytecode** → [Java Virtual Machine] → **Computer System**

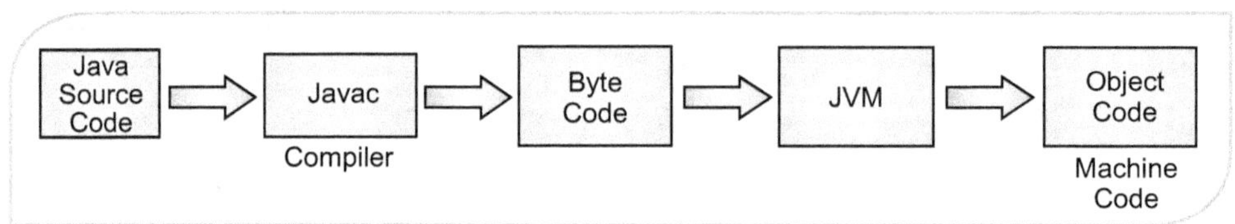

Fig. 2.2

INTRODUCTION TO BLUEJ

BlueJ is an integrated Java environment, specifically designed for introductory learning. It offers an easier way to write, compile and view Java programs.

It is being developed and maintained by a joint research group at Monash University in Melbourne, Australia and Maersk Institute at the University of Southern Denmark.

BlueJ includes :

- Project Manager
- Editor
- Compiler
- Debugger

Java is an object-oriented language. In Java, the program is written inside a class. We have to create objects of a specific class and execute the functions/methods using the object. We studied in the previous chapter about class and object. Let's see the structure of class and object.

Creating Classes in Java

A class defines user-defined objects and their characteristics. The main components of a class are :

1. Data members/variables/attributes
2. Methods

The following syntax shows how to declare a class :

Class ClassName
{
    //Declaration of data members
    // Declaration of methods
}

You can use the following code snippets to declare the Employee class that defines various data members, such as employee Name, employee ID and employee Designation.

---

2. JRE is a set of programming tools for development of Java applications.

Class Employee
{

    String employee Name;
    String employee Designation;
    int employee ID;

}

Creating Objects of Classes

An object is an instance of a class and has unique identity. The identity of an object distinguishes it from other objects. Classes and objects are closely linked to each other.

To create an object, you need to perform the following steps :

1. Declaration : Declares a variable that holds the reference to the object. The following syntax shows how :

Class_name Object_name;

2. Instantiation or creation : Creates an object of the specified class. When you declare an object, memory is not allocated to it. Therefore, you can't store data in the data members of the object. The *new* operator allocates memory to an object.

Class_name Object_name = new Class_name();

Example : Employee e1=new Employee();

The main( ) Method

The main() method is the controlling method of a program. It generally contains the initial or starting code and makes the other method calls. In BlueJ, we can execute any method by creating the objects and then right click on the desired method, that shows the main method, select it and your output will be displayed. But if we run Java code outside the BlueJ then we have to include the main method in the code i.e. public static void main (String[] args). In the following figures, can see main method inside the BlueJ & outside the BlueJ:

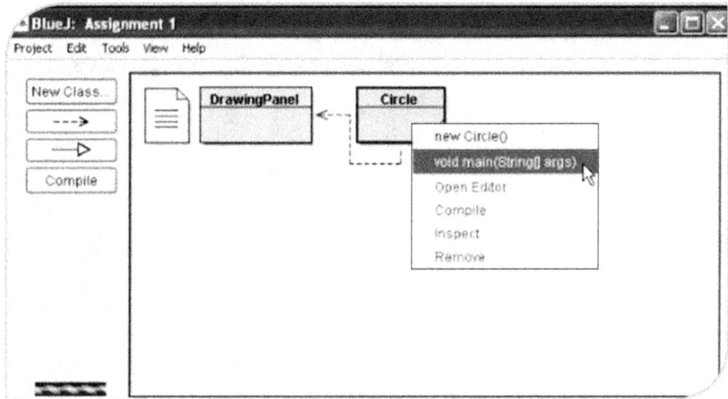

Fig. 2.3 (a)

```
class oswal
{
        public static void main(string[] args)
        {
        .........
        .....
        ...
        }
}
```

Fig. 2.3 (b)

Working of BlueJ

Now, let's understand how we can work on a Java BlueJ program :

I.   Click on the **BlueJ icon** on the start menu. It will show the BlueJ opening screen.

Fig. 2.4

II. **Click on Project → New Project,** to begin a new Project.

III. Give a name to the New Project and click on **Create**. It will be created in the specified folder [shown in **Look in**].

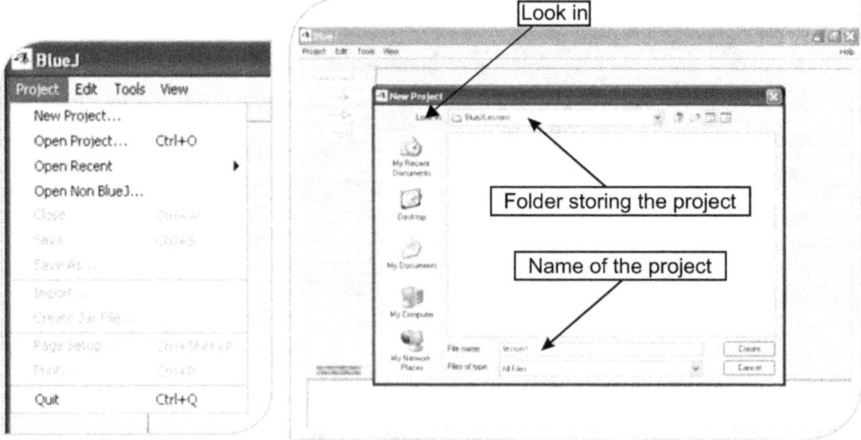

Fig. 2.5

As soon as a Project File is created, an icon appears for the Readme.txt file. It contains the description of the project. You can double click on it and fill the details. To come back to the Project window, click on Close button.

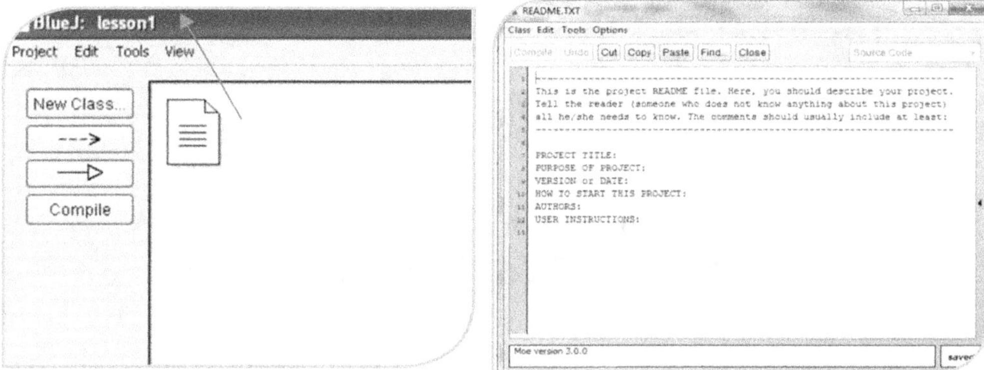

Fig. 2.6

IV. Programs are written in a class. To make a new class, click on **New Class**. A dialog box opens up. Write the name of the class and click on OK. The class icon will appear in the project window.

V. Right click on the icon. A list will appear. Choose **Open Editor**.
[You may also double click the icon to open the editor.]

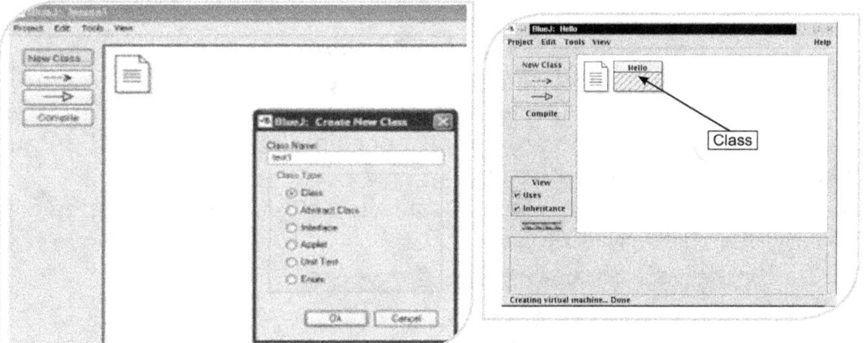

Fig. 2.7

VI. A sample program will appear with comment lines. Change this code to make your own program by adding and deleting required statements.

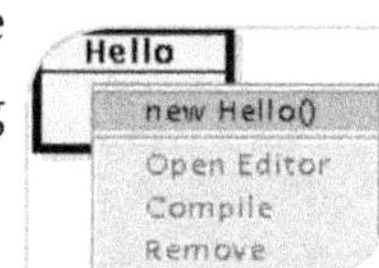

Fig. 2.8 (a) Sample Program

Fig. 2.8 (b) Modified Program

VII. Close/minimize the program window to go to the project window. Any change in the program causes stripes to reappear on the class icon. The stripes on the class icon means that the program is not compiled. A Java BlueJ program can be executed only after compilation.

VIII. To compile the program, click on compile button. The compilation is successful in case of correct syntax.

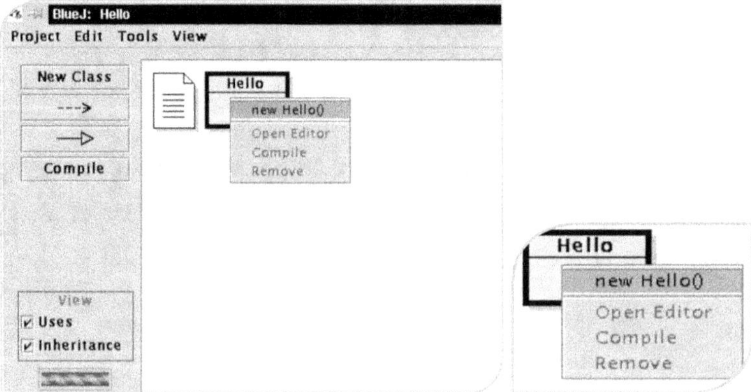

Fig. 2.9

IX. After successful compilation, the program has to be executed. Right click on the class icon and choose option 'new test1()'.

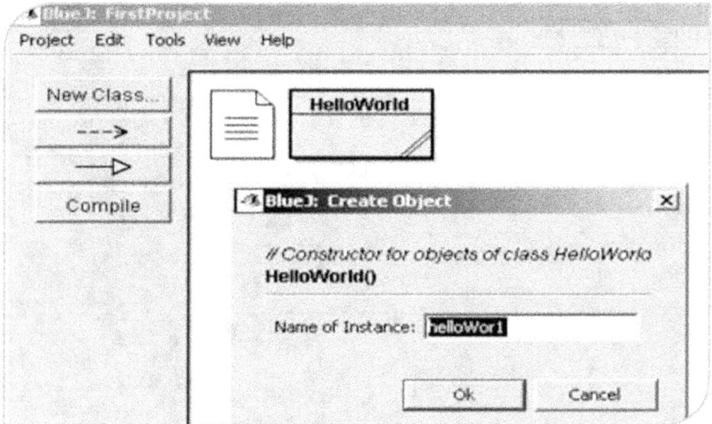

Fig. 2.10 (a)

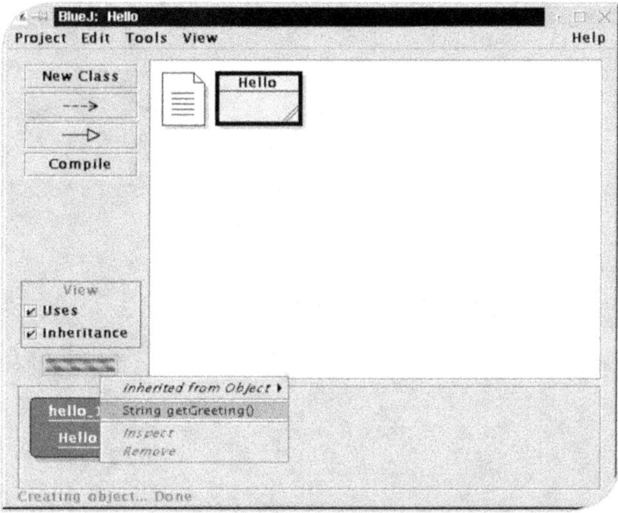

Fig. 2.10 (b)

An object is created (red rectangular box) at the left bottom of the screen. Right click on the object to get a list of methods. Click on the method to execute it.

Fig. 2.11

Executing a program – pictorial explanation : The following figure shows three vital windows of Java BlueJ. The three windows have been opened at the same time by using the restore option. Keeping the three windows open at the same time, by adjusting their sizes to fit the monitor, helps to understand the working of a program in an easier way.

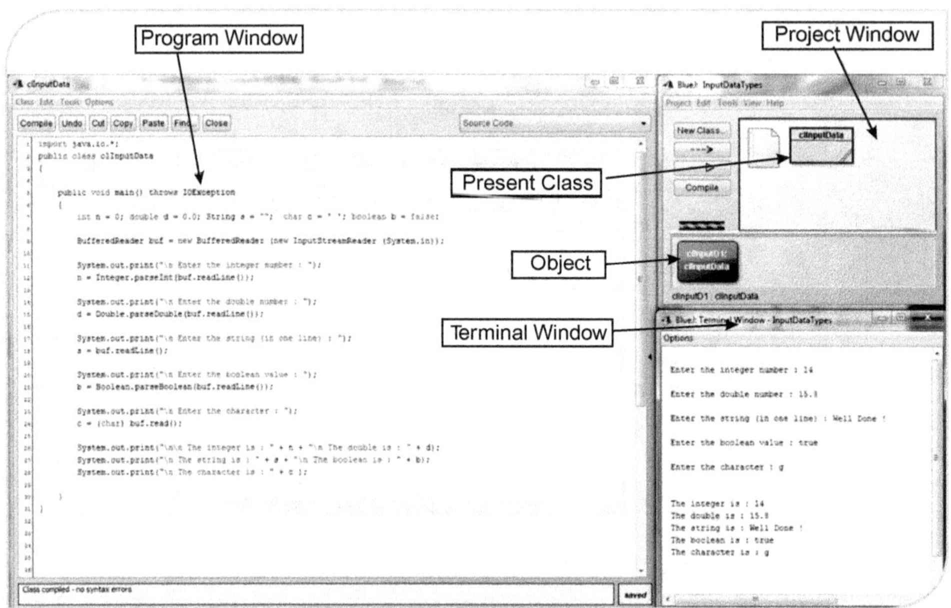

Fig. 2.12

Printing the source code in BlueJ : To print a program from BlueJ screen, click on **Class → Print**.

Documenting a Project : To prepare documentation of the project, click on **Tools → Project Documentation**

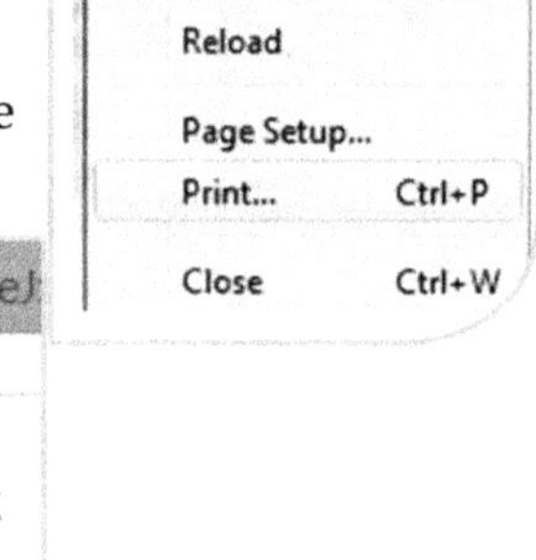

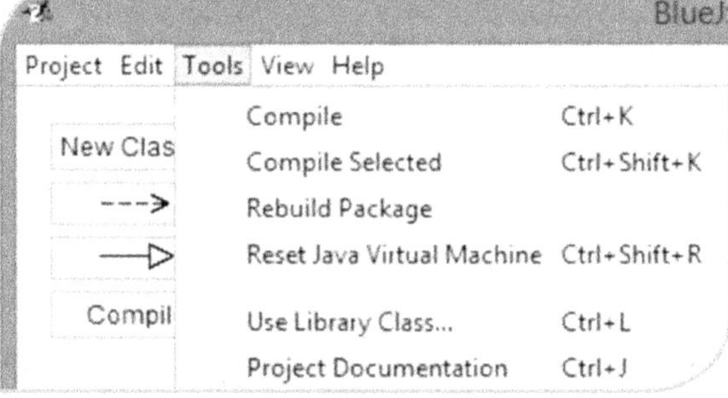

Fig. 2.13

Before we begin Java programming in detail, let us learn a **few basic terminologies**.

JAVA CHARACTER SET

It is a set of texual and graphic symbols, each of which is mapped to a set of non-negative integers.

The American Standard Code for Information Interchange (ASCII) is a character-encoding scheme that originally was based on the English alphabet. It encodes 128 specified characters into 7-bit binary integers as shown by the **ASCII** chart. It includes

English alphabets (lower and upper case), digits, symbols and special characters. ASCII code had the limitation that it was confined to a few characters and could not include further characters. To overcome the problem, extended ASCII codes were introduced. Later UNICODE was introduced which has 16 bits and could represent characters of various languages other than English.

The Unicode is an international encoding standard with different languages and scripts, by which each letter, digit, or symbol is assigned a unique numeric value that applies across different platforms and programs. Unicode allows for 17 planes, each of 65,536 possible characters (or 'code points'). This gives a total of 1,114,112 possible characters.

Dec	Hx	Oct	Char	Dec	Hx	Oct	Html	Chr	Dec	Hx	Oct	Html	Chr	Dec	Hx	Oct	Html	Chr
0	0	000	NUL (null)	32	20	040		Space	64	40	100	@	@	96	60	140	`	`
1	1	001	SOH (start of heading)	33	21	041	!	!	65	41	101	A	A	97	61	141	a	a
2	2	002	STX (start of text)	34	22	042	"	"	66	42	102	B	B	98	62	142	b	b
3	3	003	ETX (end of text)	35	23	043	#	#	67	43	103	C	C	99	63	143	c	c
4	4	004	EOT (end of transmission)	36	24	044	$	$	68	44	104	D	D	100	64	144	d	d
5	5	005	ENQ (enquiry)	37	25	045	%	%	69	45	105	E	E	101	65	145	e	e
6	6	006	ACK (acknowledge)	38	26	046	&	&	70	46	106	F	F	102	66	146	f	f
7	7	007	BEL (bell)	39	27	047	'	'	71	47	107	G	G	103	67	147	g	g
8	8	010	BS (backspace)	40	28	050	(	(	72	48	110	H	H	104	68	150	h	h
9	9	011	TAB (horizontal tab)	41	29	051	)	)	73	49	111	I	I	105	69	151	i	i
10	A	012	LF (NL line feed, new line)	42	2A	052	*	*	74	4A	112	J	J	106	6A	152	j	j
11	B	013	VT (vertical tab)	43	2B	053	+	+	75	4B	113	K	K	107	6B	153	k	k
12	C	014	FF (NP form feed, new page)	44	2C	054	,	,	76	4C	114	L	l	108	6C	154	l	l
13	D	015	CP (carriage return)	45	2D	055	-	-	77	4D	115	M	M	109	6D	155	m	m
14	E	016	SO (shift out)	46	2E	056	.	.	78	4E	116	N	N	110	6E	156	n	n
15	F	017	SI (shift in)	47	2F	057	/	/	79	4F	117	O	O	111	6F	157	o	o
16	10	020	DLE (data link escape)	48	30	060	0	0	80	50	120	P	P	112	70	160	p	p
17	11	021	DC1 (device control 1)	49	31	061	1	1	81	51	121	Q	Q	113	71	161	q	q
18	12	022	DC2 (device control 2)	50	32	062	2	2	82	52	122	R	R	114	72	162	r	r
19	13	023	DC3 (device control 3)	51	33	063	3	3	83	53	123	S	S	115	73	163	s	s
20	14	024	DC4 (device control 4)	52	34	064	4	4	84	54	124	T	T	116	74	164	t	t
21	15	025	NAK (negative acknowledge)	53	35	065	5	5	85	55	125	U	U	117	75	165	u	u
22	16	026	SYN (synchronous idle)	54	36	066	6	6	86	56	126	V	V	118	76	166	v	v
23	17	027	ETB (end of trans. block)	55	37	067	7	7	87	57	127	W	W	119	77	167	w	w
24	18	030	CAN (cancel)	56	38	070	8	8	88	58	130	X	X	120	78	170	x	x
25	19	031	EM (end of medium)	57	39	071	9	9	89	59	131	Y	Y	121	79	171	y	y
26	1A	032	SUB (substitute)	58	3A	072	:	:	90	5A	132	Z	Z	122	7A	172	z	z
27	1B	033	ESC (escape)	59	3B	073	;	;	91	5B	133	[	[	123	7B	173	{	{
28	1C	034	FS (file separator)	60	3C	074	<	<	92	5C	134	\	\	124	7C	174			|
29	1D	035	GS (group separator)	61	3D	075	=	=	93	5D	135	]	]	125	7D	175	}	}
30	1E	036	RS (record separator)	62	3E	076	>	>	94	5E	136	^	^	126	7E	176	~	~
31	1F	037	US (unit separator)	63	3F	077	?	?	95	5F	137	_	_	127	7F	177		DEL

Extended ASCII code takes the list upto 255 characters. It includes some more special characters.

Dec	Char	Dec	Char	Dec	Char	Dec	Char	Dec	Char	Dec	Char
128	Ç	151	ù	174	«	197	┼	220	▄	243	¾
129	ü	152	ÿ	175	»	198	ã	221	¦	244	¶
130	é	153	Ö	176	░	199	Ã	222	Ì	245	§
131	â	154	Ü	177	▒	200	╚	223	▀	246	÷
132	ä	155	ø	178	▓	201	╔	224	Ó	247	¸
133	à	156	£	179	│	202	╩	225	ß	248	°
134	å	157	Ø	180	┤	203	╦	226	Ô	249	¨
135	ç	158	×	181	Á	204	╠	227	Ò	250	·
136	ê	159	ƒ	182	Â	205	═	228	õ	251	¹
137	ë	160	á	183	À	206	╬	229	Õ	252	³
138	è	161	í	184	©	207	¤	230	µ	253	²
139	ï	162	ó	185	╣	208	ð	231	þ	254	■
140	î	163	ú	186	║	209	Ð	232	Þ	255	
141	ì	164	ñ	187	╗	210	Ê	233	Ú		
142	Ä	165	Ñ	188	╝	211	Ë	234	Û		
143	Å	166	ª	189	¢	212	È	235	Ù		
144	É	167	º	190	¥	213	ı	236	ý		
145	æ	168	¿	191	┐	214	Í	237	Ý		
146	Æ	169	®	192	└	215	Î	238	¯		
147	ô	170	¬	193	┴	216	Ï	239	´		
148	ö	171	½	194	┬	217	┘	240			
149	ò	172	¼	195	├	218	┌	241	±		
150	û	173	¡	196	─	219	█	242	‗		

Extended ASCII codes

EBCDIC character codes (1st hex digit across the top, 2nd hex digit down the side)

2nd hex digit	0	1	2	3	4	5	6	7	8	9	A	B	C	D	E	F
0	NUL	DLE	DS		SP	&	-									0
1	SOH	DC1	SOS				/		a	j			A	J		1
2	STX	DC2	FS	SYN					b	k	s		B	K	S	2
3	ETX	TM							c	l	t		C	L	T	3
4	PF	RES	BYP	PN					d	m	u		D	M	U	4
5	HT	NL	LF	RS					e	n	v		E	N	V	5
6	LC	BS	ETB	UC					f	o	w		F	O	W	6
7	DEL	IL	ESC	EOT					g	p	x		G	P	X	7
8		CAN							h	q	y		H	Q	Y	8
9		EM							i	r	z		I	R	Z	9
A	SMM	CC	SM		¢	!	¦	:								
B	VT	CU1	CU2	CU3	.	$	,	#								
C	FF	IFS		DC4	<	*	%	@								
D	CR	IGS	ENQ	NAK	(	)	_	'								
E	SO	IRS	ACK		+	;	>	=								
F	SI	IUS	BEL	SUB	|	¬	?	"								

EBCDIC codes

Extended Binary Coded Decimal Interchange Code (EBCDIC) is an 8-bit character encoding used mainly on IBM mainframe and IBM midrange computer operating systems.

In an EBCDIC file, each alphabetic or numeric character is represented with an 8-bit binary number (a string of eight 0's or 1's) and in this 256 possible characters (letters of the alphabet, numerals, and special characters) are defined.

ASCII and EBCDIC codes are not same. They differ in their presentation and codes of characters.

TOKEN

It is the smallest identifiable part of a program. There are five types of tokens in Java – Keywords, Identifiers, Literals, Separators and Operators.

Let us now see the details of the various tokens.

Keywords

These are words that have a specific meaning. The list of keywords used in Java is given below.

abstract	default	if	Private	this
boolean	do	implements	protected	throw
break	double	import	public	throws
byte	else	instance of	return	transient
case	extends	int	short	try
catch	final	interface	static	void
char	finally	long	strictfp	volatile
class	float	native	super	while
const	for	new	switch	
continue	goto	package	synchronized	

Identifiers

These are names given to variables, constants, classes, and methods.

Identifiers have to follow certain rules :

- The first character of an identifier must be a letter, an underscore (_), or a dollar sign($).
- The rest of the characters in the identifier can be a letter, an underscore, a dollar sign, or a digit. Note that spaces are NOT allowed in identifiers.
- Identifiers are case-sensitive. This means that *age* and *Age* are different identifiers.
- Java's keywords/reserved words cannot be used as identifiers.

Examples of Valid Identifiers : SubValue, $name, totMarks, PI, _address

Examples of Invalid Identifiers :

1. Sub Value   —   spaces are not allowed.
2. p+q   —   arithmetic operators cannot be used.
3. int   —   int is a keyword.

4. 7day   —   identifiers cannot start with a digit.

5. (week)   —   braces or any other special character other than _ and $ are not allowed.

Literals

These are constants that have a fixed value of any of the data types. They can be any number, text, or other information that represents a value.

For example, 9, 3.7 are numeric literals; 'a' is a character literal; *false* is a boolean literal.

Java has various types of literals :

Integer Literal : They hold only integers with '-' or '+' symbol. For example, 92, -6

Floating Literal : They hold real numbers that have real and fractional part, separated by a dot. For example, 83.24 , 65.12

Boolean Literal : *true* and *false* are the two reserved literal values for the boolean type.

Character Literal : In Java, a character literal is always represented by single ASCII character enclosed in a single quote. You can also have certain non graphic characters in character constants in Java. Non graphic characters are those which are not readily typed using a keyboard such as tabs, backspace, etc. However, with the use of an escape sequence, these types of characters can be represented. An escape sequence is symbolized with a special syntax, which starts with a backslash (\) character followed by one or more characters.

Escape Sequence	Meaning	Escape Sequence	Meaning
\a	Audible bell (alert)	\r	Carriage return
\b	Backspace	\ ?	Question mark
\n	New line	\ 0n	Shows the number in octal form
\f	Form feed		
\v	Vertical tab	\ xHn	Shows the number in hexadecimal form
\t	Horizontal tab		
\\	Backslash	\uHn	Unicode characters are represented using its hexadecimal code Hn.
\'	Single quote		
\"	Double quote	\0	Null

The above table shows sequences representing \, ', " and ? also. The mentioned characters can be typed with the help of a keyboard but when they are used without an escape sequence, they carry a special purpose and meaning. If you want to type these characters as they are, then you should use escape sequences. Given below are the examples of character literals :

'a', '%', '\t', '\\', '\"', '\288', 'Ω', etc.

String Literal : They consist of a range of characters enclosed in double quotes (" "). For example, "salvadore", "qatar",

Null Literal : The null literal has only one value, written as 'null'. For example, a = null;

Punctuators

The following nine ASCII characters are the punctuators (separators) in Java:

( )   { }   [ ]   ;   ,   .

Note :

; is also called a statement terminator.

Operators

These are special symbols that perform specific operations on one, two, or three operands, and then return a result. We can divide all the Java operators into the following groups : [*in detail, we will discuss in next chapter*]

- Arithmetic Operators
- Relational Operators
- Bitwise Operators
- Logical Operators
- Assignment Operators
- Misc Operators

CONSTANTS & VARIABLES

Constant

A constant is a value that cannot be changed.

- Examples of integer constants:
  354, -37, 0, 246543 .
- Examples of floating point constants:
  4.642, -0.034, 5.98e24 (mass of earth), 9.11e-31 (mass of electron)
- Examples of character constants:
  'A', 'y', '8', '*', ' ' (space), '\n' (new line).

Variable

A variable is a piece of memory that can contain a data value. It has these attributes :

- **Name :** The string of letters in a program used to designate a variable.
  A name should start with a letter and consist of letters and/or digits.
  Variables in names are case sensitive (capitalization matters).
  The naming convention in Java is to start a variable name with a lower case letter. New words within a name start with a capital letter.
  (**example** : numberOfCustomers).
- **Value :** The binary data contained in memory. The value is interpreted according to the variable's datatype.
- **Address :** The location in memory where the value is stored.
- **Size :** The number of bytes that the variable occupies in memory.

- **Datatype :** The interpretation of the value.
- **Range :** The minimum and maximum values of the variable. The range of a variable depends on its size. In general, the bigger the size in bytes, the bigger the range.

Example variable declarations :

int maxAge;

int x, y, selectedIndex;

char a, b;

boolean flag;

double maxVal, massInKilos;

DATA TYPES

Data types define the type of the data. Java provides two types of data types :

Primitive data types are readily available for programmer's use. Java has eight primitive data types, which are boolean, char, byte, short, int, long, float, double. Examples : int v = 5; double d = 2.9;

Composite data types are generally made up of multiple primitive data types. Java provides two composite data types classes and arrays. Example of composite data type :

class Student

{

    String name; int age; double marks ;

}

Student sm;

Here, Student is a class and sm is an object (member data). Class Student can have any combination of member data which may be String name, int age, double marks, etc.

Data Variables and their types : Variables are the named units that store values of a specific type. Following are some important data types :

Variable Type	Description	Size	Example	Value Range (including both limits)
byte	Byte length integer	1 byte	byte b = 2;	-128 to +127
short	Short integer whole numbers	2 bytes	short s = 7;	-32,768 to +32767
int	Integer whole numbers	4 bytes	int x = 5;	-2^{31} to $+2^{31}-1$
long	Bigger integer whole numbers	8 bytes	long n = 980807465	-2^{63} to $+2^{63}-1$
float	Fractional numbers	4 bytes	float f = 45.7	-3.4×10^{-38} to $+3.4 \times 10^{38} -1$
double	Bigger fractional numbers	8 bytes	double d = 72.889344265534	-1.7×10^{308} to $+1.7 \times 10^{308}-1$

char	Keyboard characters	16 bits Unicode	char h = 'd'	'\u0000' or 0 '\uffff' or 65,535
boolean	Values of type True or False	1 byte	boolean st = false	0 1

Statement : It is the smallest unit of a program that gets executed. Statements in Java are terminated by a semicolon (;).

Block : A group of statements that have a specific aim is called a block. They are used to divide a big task into smaller tasks. It helps in understanding bigger problems. Blocks are generally enclosed within a pair of parenthesis (second bracket { }).

Type Casting

It is the process by which we can convert one data type to another data type. Casting is important in some situations when we have a return value from a method in one type and the manipulation on the value has to be done in another data type. The type castings can be carried out automatically (implicit) or forced (explicit).

The casting is performed by keeping the target data type in parentheses to the left of the value which is converted.

Syntax :

dataType variableName = (dataType) variableToConvert;

Example

double calculated Mark = 85.6;

int final Grade = (int)calculatedMark; //will return 85

In Java, type casting is classified into two types,

1. Implicit Casting (Widening)

In this kind of type conversion, the resulting data types are not specified and are chosen by the compiler. The compiler prefers not to lose any part of data value.

$$\text{byte} \rightarrow \text{short} \rightarrow \text{int} \rightarrow \text{long} \rightarrow \text{float} \rightarrow \text{double}$$

Implicit

2. Explicit Casting(Narrowing)

In this kind of type conversion, the resulting data types are explicitly specified by the programmer.

$$\text{double} \rightarrow \text{float} \rightarrow \text{long} \rightarrow \text{int} \rightarrow \text{short} \rightarrow \text{byte}$$

Explicit

The following table shows the numeric data types and their allowed type conversions.

Data type from	Data type to	I – Implicit E – Explicit
short	int/long/float/double	I
int	long/float/double	I
	short	E

long	int/float	E
	double	I
float	short/int	E
	long/double	I
double	short/int/long/float	E

Method of Type Casting

To convert the data type of a variable to another type, the target data type has to be written in front within brackets.

Syntax : (target data type)V; // V is the variable/value

Syntaxes of explicit and implicit type casting

(i)   int k = 25.69 ;   // not allowed by the compiler, syntax error "possible loss of precision"

(ii) int r = 10;
      double n = 15.26 ;
      *r = n ;   // data-type of **r** is lower than **n**
      // not allowed by the compiler, syntax error   "possible loss of precision"

(iii) double k = 65 ; // allowed by the compiler

(iv) double n = 75.63 ;
      int r = 48 ;
      n = r ;   // allowed by the compiler, since the data-type of **n** is higher than *r*

(v) int r = 37;
      double n = 92.64 ;
      r = (int) n ;   // allowed by the compiler
                         //explicit type casting of n, it truncates the fractional part of n

---

Example 1 :

```
class DataType
{
    void main( )
    {
        int t = (int)25.75;
        System.out.println(" Value of t = " + t );
        int c = 'a';
        System.out.println(" Value of c = " + c );
        double d = 45;
        System.out.println(" Value of d = " + d);
    }
}
```

Output

Value of t = 25
Value of c = 97
Value of d = 45.0

Example 2 :

```
class DataType
{
    void main( )
    {
```

```
        int p = 10, q = 20;
        long c = 9876, d = 5432;
        c = p; // allowed by compiler
        q = d;// Error, not allowed by compiler
        q = (int)d;// allowed, explicit type conversion
    }
}
```

SUMMARY

- A Java Applet is a small and efficient Java program, which is used for internet programming. Applets are typically executed in an AppletViewer.
- Java Application is a Java program that has an aim and can be executed as a single program.
- Java code is compiled to create Java bytecode which is processed by Java virtual machine.
- The portability or machine independence of a Java program is because of the Java Byte Code.
- Java virtual machine is a software that converts Java byte code to machine language.
- Java BlueJ is an integrated Java environment specifically designed for introductory learning. It includes Project Manager, Editor, Compiler, Debugger.
- ASCII encodes 128 specified characters into 7-bit binary integers.
- Unicode allows for 17 planes, each of 65,536 possible characters (or 'code points').
- **Token** : It is the smallest identifiable part of a program. Tokens in Java are – Keywords, Identifiers, Literals, Separators and Operators.
- **Keywords** are words that have a specific meaning.
- **Identifiers** are names given to variables, constants, classes, and methods. Keywords cannot be used as identifiers.
- Identifiers have to follow certain rules :
  - The first character of an identifier must be a letter, an underscore (_), or a dollar sign($).
  - The rest of the characters in the identifier can be a letter, an underscore, a dollar sign, or a digit. Note that spaces are NOT allowed in identifiers.
  - Identifiers are case-sensitive. This means that *age* and *Age* are different identifiers.
  - Java's keywords/reserved words cannot be used as identifiers.
- **Literals** : These are constants that have a fixed value. For example – 9, 3.7
- **Punctuators :** The following nine ASCII characters are the Java punctuators (*separators*). ( ) { } [ ] ;   ,   .
- **Statement** : It is the smallest unit of a program that gets executed. Statements in Java are terminated by a semicolon (;).
- **Block** : A group of statements that have a specific aim is called a block. They are used to divide a big task into smaller tasks. It helps in understanding bigger problems. Blocks are generally enclosed within a pair of parenthesis (second bracket { }).

- **Type Casting :** It is the conversion of data from one type to another.
  - ◆ **Explicit Type Conversion** : Data types are explicitly specified by the programmer.
  - ◆ **Implicit Type Conversion** : Data types are not specified and are chosen by the compiler. This kind of type conversion causes no data loss.
- **Operators** are special symbols that perform specific operations on one, two, or three *operands,* and then return a result.
  - ◆ Assignment Operator
  - ◆ Increment/Decrement Operator
  - ◆ Arithmetic Operators
  - ◆ Relational Operators
  - ◆ Misc Operators
- A constant is a value that cannot be changed.
- A variable is a piece of memory that can contain a data value.

SOLVED QUESTIONS

1. **Write the important features of Java.**

   Answer :

   I. **Platform Independent :** Programs written in Java can be executed on any other platform (such as Windows, Unix, Linux, Mac OS, etc) that has the Java virtual machine (JVM).

   II. **Portable :** The feature of Platform Independence makes a Java program portable and follows the concept "Write Once Run Anywhere (WORA)".

   III. **Object-Oriented :** Java is an OOPL that supports the construction of programs that consist of collections of collaborating objects. These objects have a unique identity, encapsulate attributes and operations, and are instances of classes related by inheritance and polymorphism.

   IV. **Simple :** Java was designed with a small number of language constructs so that programmers could learn it quickly. It eliminates several language features available in C/C++ that are associated with poor programming practices or are rarely used.

   V. **Secure :** Java is designed to be secure in a networked environment. The Java run-time environment uses a bytecode verification process to ensure tat code loaded over the network does not violate Java security constraints.

   VI. **Robust :** Java is designed to eliminate certain types of programming errors. Java is strongly typed, which allows extensive compile-time error checking. It does not support memory pointers, which eliminates the possibility of overwriting memory and corrupting data. In addition, its automatic memory management (garbage collection) eliminates memory leaks and other problems associated with dynamic memory allocation/de-allocation.

   VII. **Wide Application Area :** Java programming language can be used in developing programs of various kinds. It is also used in a variety of devices for implementing solutions such as networking of PCs, the Internet, mobile and entertainment software, etc.

2. **What is Java Bytecode ?**

   Answer : Java code is compiled to create Java bytecode which is processed by Java virtual machine. This code is independent of the processor of the computer system. The portability or machine independence of a Java program is because of this Java byte code.

3. **What is type casting ?**

   Answer : Type Casting is the conversion of data from one type to another.
   - **Explicit Type Conversion :** Data types are explicitly specified by the programmer.
   - **Implicit Type Conversion :** Data types are not specified and are chosen by the compiler. This kind of type conversion causes no data loss.

4. **Define JAVA applets.**

   Answer. Java applets are compiled Java programs which are run through a web browser.

5. **What is Object Code ?**

   Answer. This object code is closest to machine code and the Java compiler generates the corresponding machine language.

EXERCISE

Question 1 : Fill in the blanks :

(a) .... is also called a statement terminator.

(b) The symbol of assignment operator is ....

(c) A character literal is always represents by .... ASCII character.

(d) The smallest identifiable part of a program is called ....

(e) The main () method is the .... method of a program.

Question 2 : Write the difference between the following and give example :

(a) Explicit   &   Implicit Conversion.

(b) Keyword   &   Identifier

(c) Primitive   &   Non-Primitive data types.

(d) Short   &   int

(e) Boolen   &   Character Literal

Question 3 : State true or false :

(a) Conversion data-type int to double is Implicit.

(b) Conversion data-type double to int is also Implicit.

(c) Data type of '/n' is integer.

(d) Java compiler can detect runtime error.

(e) To convert the data type of a variable to another type, the target data type has to be written in front within brackets.

Question 4 : Answer the following in brief :

(a) What is token ?

(b) What is a literal ?

(c) What is a statement ?

(d) What are the rules that identifiers must follow ?

(e) Name the Java Relational Operators and their function.

Chapter 3

OPERATORS IN JAVA

Contents
- Operators in Java
  - ❖ Forms of Operators – Unary, Binary, Ternary
  - ❖ Types of Operators
    - ◆ Assignment
    - ◆ Arithmetic
    - ◆ Relational
    - ◆ Logical
    - ◆ Increment/Decrement(Prefix and Postfix)
    - ◆ Shorthand
- Counter & Accumulator
- Hierarchy of Operators
  - ❖ Precedence
  - ❖ Associativity
- Keyword 'new'
- Referencing Operator ('.' dot operator)
- Printing Statements
- Summary
- Solved Questions
- Exercise

OPERATORS IN JAVA

An **operator** is a symbol that indicates the operation of a task involving operands. There are different forms and types of operators that return some result upon completion of their operation.

Forms of Operators

Operators get operated on operands. The forms of operators are Unary (one operand), Binary (two operands), Ternary (three operands).

Unary

Unary operator takes only one value for its operation. For example, unary + , unary - , increment (++) and decrement(- -)

+ 9 , - 45

a + + , - - d   where a, d are variables

Binary

A binary operator takes two operands and calculates a result to return. For example, the arithmetic operators commonly used for calculations such as

+   -   *   /   %

a + 6 ,   p * q   etc

Ternary

A ternary operator takes three operands and returns accordingly. Java uses ternary operator for small conditional values.

int d = (a>b) ? a : b ;

[*In detail we will discuss in the chapter of Conditional Statements*]

Types of Operators

There are many types of operators in Java which are used for various types of calculations and decision making purposes. Let us look at the types of operators in the following section :

Simple Assignment Operator

=   Simple assignment operator

This operator is used for assigning value to a variable. It operates on right to left direction. It does not permit any constant on its left side.

c = 9   It assigns value 9 in variable c.

3 = a   It causes error, since there is a constant 3 on the left side

This operator also permits overwriting of a variable on itself.

a = 4

a = a + 1   It causes a to become 5 by using its own previous value which was 4

Arithmetic Operators

These are similar to the mathematical operators except for % operator.

+   Additive operator to give the sum

-     Subtraction operator to give the difference

*   Multiplication operator to give the product

/   Division operator to give the quotient

%   Remainder operator (% is called Modulus) to give the remainder

Note :

- % or Modulus operator works only on integers.

  Arithmetic operators are binary operators as they need two operands.

Relational Operators

These operators are used for conditional verifications. They give result in either a True or a False.

==	Equal to
!=	Not equal to
>	Greater than
>=	Greater than or equal to
<	Less than
<=	Less than or equal to

Examples :

Operator	Example
= =	5 == 3 is evaluated to false
!=	5 != 3 is evaluated to true
>	5 > 3 is evaluated to true
<	5 < 3 is evaluated to false
>=	5 >= 5 is evaluated to true
<=	7<= 5 is evaluated to false

Logical Operators

A **logical operator** is sometimes called a "Boolean operator". These operators are used on conditions. Two of them are used for connecting conditions and one is used for negating a condition. They give result in either a True or a False.

Sometimes, expressions that use logical operators are called "compound expressions" because they combine two or more condition tests into a single expression.

!   **NOT**

It is applicable on one condition and it returns the negated result of the condition

&&   **AND**

It is applicable on two conditions and it returns True only if the result of both the conditions is True

| | **OR**

It is applicable on two conditions and it returns True if the result of any of the conditions is True

Increment/Decrement Operator with Prefix and Postfix

These operators are used for increasing or decreasing the value of a variable by 1. There are two forms of these operators: **prefix** and **postfix.**

++ Increment operator

- It increases the value of a variable by 1.
- If applied as prefix then at first the variable's value increases and is used.
- If applied as postfix then at first the variable's value is used and then is incremented.

d = 6;

d++ ;   // it makes the value of d = 7

--   **Decrement operator**

- It decreases the value of a variable by 1.
- If applied as prefix then at first the variable's value decreases and is used.
- If applied as postfix then at first the variable's value is used and then is decremented.

```
m = 4;
- -m ;          // it makes the value of m = 3
```

Also note the following examples for post and pre increment/decrement operations.

```
a = 5;
b = a++;     // it makes b = 5 , a = 6
p = 7;
q = ++p ;    // it makes q = 8 , p = 8
```

Applictaions of Increment/decrement Operators

Code 1	`p = 30;`	
	`r = p ++;`	`// r = 30  & p = 31`
Code 2	`p = 40;`	
	`r = ++p ;`	`// r = 41 & p = 41`
Code 3	`p = 10;`	
	`r = p ++ + p ;`	`// r = 10 + 11 = 21  & p = 11`
Code 4	`p = 120; q = 110;`	
	`r = p -- + q-- ;`	`// r = 120 + 110 = 130 & p = 119 , q = 109`
Code 5	`p = 201; q = 101;`	
	`r = --p + --q ;`	`// r = 200 + 100 = 300& p = 200 , q = 100`
Code 6	`p = 25;`	
	`p = p++ + ++p ;`	`// p = 25 + 27 = 52`
Code 7	`p = 5;`	
	`p+= p++ ;`	`// p = p + (p++);  p = 5 + 5 = 10` `// no effect of p++ here`
Code 8	`p = 5;`	

	`p+= (p++) ;`	`// p = p + (p++);  p = 5 + 5 = 10`
		`// no effect of (p++) here, 5 +6 does`
		`not take place`

Code 9	`p = 7;`	
	`p+= p++ * 2;`	`// p = p + (p++ * 2);  p = 7 + (7*2) = 21`
Code 10	`p = 5;`	
	`p+= p ++ + ++p ;`	`// p = p+ (p++ + ++p) = 5 + ( 5 + 7) = 17`
Code 11	`q = 4;`	
	`q-= (--q * q++) ;`	`// q = q - ( --q * q++) = 4 – (3 * 3) = –5`
Code 12	`w = 7; q = 9;`	
	`d = (--w*q++ - q*--w) ;`	`// d = 6*9 – 10*5 = 72 – 50 = 22`

Shorthand Operator

These are a combination of arithmetic operator and assignment operator. They are of the form **N op=V** where N is a variable, V is value of modification, op is Java binary operator and **op=** is called shorthand operator. They are explained in the table below :

Shorthand operator	Equivalent statement using Assignment operator
N+=5	N = N + 5
N−=4	N = N - 4
N*=k	N = N * k, k is another variable
N/=m	N = N / m, m is another variable
N%=p	N = N % p, p is another variable

Examples :
(i)   int   R = 12;
    R += 5 ;
    System.out.print("Result = " + R) ;   // R = 17
(ii) double   K = 36.6 ;
    K /= 2 ;
    System.out.print("Final value = " + K) ;   // K = 18.3
(iii) int P = 10 ;
    P *= 2 ;
    System.out.println(" Value of P = " + P);   // P = 20
(iv) double D = 2.5 , c = 3.4;
    D += c;
    System.out.println(" Value of D = " + D);   // D = 5.9

COUNTER AND ACCUMULATOR

A **counter** is a variable that is used for counting. It increases by a fixed value.
A common place of its use is in a loop as a loop counter.
For example :
for (int k = 1; k<=10; k++) // k is a counter [a loop counter]

Note :
- The value of k is expressing by 1 each time.

An **accumulator** is a variable that is used for accumulating or storing a result formed by accumulation. It gets modified by some unknown value.
For example :

```
int sum = 0;
for (int k = 1; k<=10; k++)
{
        sum = sum + k ;
}
System.out.print( " Sum is " + k );
```

Note :

- The value of sum is changing by variable k, which is different each time.
  An interesting way of expressing counter and accumulator is :

  - A counter tells how many.
  - An accumulator tells how much.

  [*We will discuss about application of counters and accumulators in the later chapters*]

HIERARCHY OF OPERATORS

Java has well-defined rules for speci-fying the order in which the operators in an expression are evaluated when the expression has several operators. For example, multiplication and division have a higher precedence than addition and subtraction. Precedence rules can be overridden by explicit parentheses.

Precedence /Priority : When more than one operator is present in an expression, the operator having higher precedence/priority get operated first.

Associativity : When more than one operator of same precedence is present, an expression gets evaluated according to their associativity.

Given below is the priority chart from highest to lowest :

Precedence	Operator	Type	Associativity
11	() [ ].	Parentheses Array subscript Member selection	Left to Right
10	++ --	Unary post- increment Unary post-decrement	Right to left
9	++ -- + - !	Unary pre-increment Unary pre-decrement Unary plus Unary minus Unary logical negation	Right to left
8	* / %	Multiplication Division Modulus	Left to right
7	+ -	Addition Subtraction	Left to right
6	< <= > >=	Relational less than Relational less than or equal Relational greater than Relational greater than or equal	Left to right
5	== !=	Relational is equal to Relational is not equal to	Left to right
4	&&	Logical AND	Left to right
3	||	Logical OR	Left to right

2	? :	Ternary conditional	Right to left
1	= += -= *= /= %=	Assignment Addition assignment Subtraction assignment Multiplication assignment Division assignment Modulus assignment	Right to left

Examples

(i) $\quad 5 + 4*3 = 5 + (4*3)$ $\qquad\qquad\quad = 17$	(ii) $\quad 11 - 8 - 5 = (11 - 8) - 5$ $\qquad\qquad\qquad = (3) - 5$ $\qquad\qquad\qquad = -2$
(iii) $\quad 5 * 4 + 3 = (5*4) + 3$ $\qquad\qquad\quad = 23$	(iv) $\quad 11 - (8 - 5) = 11 - (3)$ $\qquad\qquad\qquad = 8$
(v) $\quad 5*2 + 20/2 = (5*2) + (20/2)$ $\qquad\qquad\qquad = 10 + 10$ $\qquad\qquad\qquad = 20$	(vi) $\quad 19 + 6/3 + 2 = 19 + (6/3) + 2$ $\qquad\qquad\qquad = 19 + 2 + 2$ $\qquad\qquad\qquad = 23$
(vii) $\quad 25\%16\%10 = (25\%16)\%10$ $\qquad\qquad\qquad = 9\%10$ $\qquad\qquad\qquad = 9$	(viii) $(19+6)/(3+2) = (25)/(5)$ $\qquad\qquad\qquad = 5$
(ix) $\quad 25\%(16\%10) = 25\%6$ $\qquad\qquad\qquad = 1$	(x) $(18 + 6)/3 + 2 = 24/3 + 2$ $\qquad\qquad\qquad = (24/3) + 2$ $\qquad\qquad\qquad = 8 + 2$ $\qquad\qquad\qquad = 10$
(xi) $\quad 50/5*2 = 10*2$ $\qquad\qquad\qquad = 20$	(xii) $\quad a = b = c = 6$ $\rightarrow \quad a = (b = (c = 6))$ $\rightarrow \quad$ Making a, b, c all 6
(xiii) $\quad 50*5/10 = 250/10$ $\qquad\qquad\qquad = 25$	(xiv) $\quad 5 + 30\%7 = 5 + (30\%7)$ $\qquad\qquad\qquad = 5 + (2)$ $\qquad\qquad\qquad = 7$
(xv) $\quad (6 + 30)\%8 = 36\%8$ $\qquad\qquad\qquad = 4$	(xvi) $\quad 6245\%5 + 2330\%10$ $\qquad\qquad\qquad = (6245\%5) + (2330\%10)$ $\qquad\qquad\qquad = 0 + 0 = 0$
(xvii) $52 + (35\%(24/(9 - 5)))$ $\qquad\qquad = 52 + (35\%(24/(4)))$ $\qquad\qquad = 52 + (35\%(6))$ $\qquad\qquad = 52 + 5$ $\qquad\qquad = 57$	(xviii) $(95 - 45/5*5)/2$ $\qquad\qquad = (95 - (45/5)*5)/2$ $\qquad\qquad = (95 - 9*5)/2$ $\qquad\qquad = (95 - (9*5))/2$ $\qquad\qquad = (95 - 45)/2$ $\qquad\qquad = (50)/2$ $\qquad\qquad = 25$

More Examples :

void T()	**Output**
{	Result R1 = 12.0
double R1 = 25 * 2/4;	Result R2 = 0.0
System.out.println(" Result R1 = " + R1);	Result R3 = 12.5
double R2 = 2/4 * 25;	Result R4 = 12.5
System.out.println(" Result R2 = " + R2);	**Reason :**
double R3 = 2.0/4 * 25;	The value of the result changes
System.out.println(" Result R3 = " + R3);	because of typecasting.
double R4 = (double)2/4 * 25 ;	
System.out.println(" Result R4 = " + R4);	
}	

Note :

- The special case of Integer Division.

Incase of integer division, the result becomes an integer. Observe the following examples :

```
c = 6/10 ;    c becomes 0
d = 6.0/10 ;  d becomes 0.6
p = 12/8 ;    p becomes 1
q = 12/8.0 ;  q becomes 1.5
```

NEW OPERATOR

Keyword *new* is used to allocate memory to an object at runtime. Such memory allocation is called dynamic memory allocation.

In case of composite data types, memory requirement is not fixed as in case of primitive data type. Size of composite data types can vary from one to another. The compiler therefore cannot allot a predefined memory to objects of these kinds. Keyword new is used to allot memory area depending on the present size of an object.

Example 1 : int ar[ ] = new int [5];

Example 2 : Student sm = new Student( );

REFERENCING OPERATOR
('.' DOT OPERATOR)

Dot ( ) operator is used to access elements/members of an object through its class name or reference variable.

Example 1 : Math.pow(5, 3);

Here, we are accessing method **pow** of class **Math**.

Example 2 : System.out.print("Hello") ;

To print the data on the monitor, we use dot operator between 'System' and 'out' in the statements. System is the name of a class included in every Java implementation. It has an object reference variable that points to a *PrintStream* object for the monitor. So, System.out.print ("Hello") invokes the print() method of the System.out object.

PRINTING STATEMENTS

System.out.print( ) : This statement prints the argument inside the bracket and then the cursor waits at the end of the printed sentence.

System.out.println( ) : This statement prints the argument inside the bracket and then the cursor waits in the next line after the printed sentence. The 'ln' is for giving a new line after the print.

Simple Programs Applying Printing Statements

Example 1 : Application of statement System.out.print ( ).

```
import java.io.*;
public class Sample
{
    public void main()
    {
        System.out.print (" ARUNACHAL PRADESH ");
        System.out.print (" HIMACHAL PRADESH ");
        System.out.print (" MADHYA PRADESH ");
        System.out.print (" UTTAR PRADESH ");
    }
}
```

OUTPUT

ARUNACHAL PRADESH HIMACHAL PRADESH MADHYA PRADESH UTTAR PRADESH

Example 2 : Application of statement System.out.println ( ). After each print statement here a new line is getting printed.

```
import java.io.*;
public class Sample
{
    public void main()
    {
        System.out.println (" ARUNACHAL PRADESH ");
        System.out.println (" HIMACHAL PRADESH ");
        System.out.println (" MADHYA PRADESH ");
        System.out.println (" UTTAR PRADESH ");
    }
}
```

OUTPUT

ARUNACHAL PRADESH
HIMACHAL PRADESH

MADHYA PRADESH
UTTAR PRADESH
[More application of output is in the next chapters]

SUMMARY

- An operator that takes only one value for its operation is known as **Unary** operator.
- A **Binary** operator operates on two operands and returns a result
- Any operator is used on three operands or variable is known as **Ternary**.
- The conditional operator or **ternary operator**(?:) is shorthand for if-then-else statement. The syntax of conditional operator is:
  variable = Condition ? True expression1 :False expression2 ;
- **Arithmetic operators** are similar to the mathematical operators except for % operator.
- A **relational operator** compares two values and determines the relationship between them.
- A **logical operator** (sometimes called a "Boolean operator") are used on conditions. Two of them(&& and | |) are used for connecting conditions and one of them (!) is used for negating a condition. They give result in either a True or a False.
- **Increment/Decrement operators** are used for increasing or decreasing the value of a variable by 1. There are two forms of these operators : prefix and postfix.
- **Shorthand Operators** are a combination of arithmetic operator and assignment operator.
- When more than one operator is present in an expression, the operator having higher **precedence / priority** get operated first.
- When more than one operator of same precedence is present, an expression gets evaluated according to their **associativity**.
- Java allows to dynamically allocate memory at run time for newly created objects or arrays using the **new** keyword
- . **(dot)** operator is used to access elements/members of an object through its reference variable.
- System.out.print( ) : This statement prints the argument inside the bracket and then the cursor waits at the end of the printed sentence.
- System.out.println( ) : This statement prints the argument inside the bracket and then the cursor waits in the next line after the printed sentence. The 'ln' is for giving a new line after the print.

SOLVED QUESTIONS

1. **What are Relational Operators ?**

   Answer. These operators are used in conditions. They are :

   Relational Operators

==	Equal to
!=	Not equal to

>	Greater than
>=	Greater than or equal to
<	Less than
<=	Less than or equal to

2. **What is precedence or priority? What is associativity ?**

   Answer. Precedence : When more than one operator is present in an expression, the operator having higher precedence / priority get operated first.

   Associativity : When more than one operator of same precedence is present, an expression gets evaluated according to their associativity.

3. **What are increment and decrement operators ?**

   Answer. These operators are a short form of simple assignment operator.

   Increment operator '++' is used to increase the value of a variable by 1.

   Similarly decrement operator '– –' decreases the value of a variable by 1.

4. **What is the use of 'new' operator ?**

   Answer. Keyword *new* is used to allocate memory to an object at runtime. Such memory allocation is called dynamic memory allocation.

5. **What is the use of ' .' dot operator ?**

   Answer. Dot ( ) operator is used to access elements/members of an object through its class name or reference variable.

6. **What will be the final value of the variables in the following codes**

   (i)   int k = 12, b = 0 ;

   b = – –k + k– – ;

   Ans. b = 11 + 11 = 22; k = 10

   (ii)   int w = 7, m = 9 ;

   m = m++ + ++w ;

   Ans. m = 9 + 8 = 17; w = 8;   Note: m++ has no effect on m

   (iii)   int v = 100, a = 0 ;

   a = v + v ++ + ++v ;

   Ans. a = 100 + 100 + 102 = 302; v = 102

   (iv)   int p = 11, q = 21, b = 0;

   b = – –p + – –q + p++ + q++ ;

   Ans. b = 10 + 20 + 10 + 20 = 60; p = 11, q = 21

   (v)   int d= 75,b = 25, r = 9;

   r = ++r + d – – + b – – ;

   Ans. r = 10 + 75 + 25 = 60; d = 74, b = 24;

   Note : ++r is used in calculation but is overwritten finally

   (v)   int f= 6, g = 3, h = 8 ;

   h += f++ + ++g ;

   Ans. h = h + (f++ + ++g) = 8 + (6 + 4) = 18 ; f = 5 , g = 4

   (vii)   int s= 99,q = 50 , r = 2 ;

   r *= ++s - q-- ;

   Ans. r = r *(++s –q– –) = 2 * (100 – 50) = 100; s = 100, q = 49

(viii) int k = 16 ,g = 6 , p = 15 ;

     p –= – –k – – – g ;

Ans. p = p-(– –k + – –g) = 15 – (15 – 5) = 5

(ix) double da = 12.5 ,   db = 0.5 , dc = 0.5 ;

     dc= da-- + db++ ;

Ans. dc = 13.0 , da = 11.5 , db = 0.5

(x) double p = 17.12 ,   q = 0.08 , r = 0;

     r += ++p – ++q;

Ans. r = 17.04, p = 18.12, q = 1.08

EXERCISE

Question 1 : Answer the following in brief :

(a) What is an operator ?

(b) What are unary, binary & ternary operators ?

(c) What are the types of operator ?

(d) What is a shorthand operator ?

(e) What is precedence of operators ?

Question 2 : Write the difference between the following and give examples :

(a) System.out.print( ) & System.out.println( )

(b) Increment operator & Decrement operator

(c) Assignment operator & Relational operator of equality

(d) Counter & Accumulator

(e) new operator & dot operator

Question 3 : State true or false :

(a) (a>= b)   when   a = 15, b = 25

(b) (a<= b)   when   a = 10, b = 10

(c) (p != q)   when   p = 9, q = 9

(d) (p== q)   when   p = 3325, q = 3325

(e) (m<n)   when   m = 64, n = 75

Question 4 : Fill in the blanks :

(a) Logical operator _____ is applicable on one condition.

(b) If decrement operator is applied as _____ then at first the variable's value decreases and then the value is used.

(c) _____ operator also permits overwriting of a variable on itself.

(d) _____ operator result in either a True or a False.

(e) An _____ gets modified by some unknown value.

INPUT IN JAVA

Content
- Value in a variable
- Initialization – data before execution
- Parameter
- Packages
- Input / Output
    - ❖ Input Stream (Scanner class)
- Errors in a Program
- Comments
- Mathematical Library Methods
- Java Expression – using all the operators and methods of Math class
- Summary
- Solved Questions
- Exercise

VALUE IN A VARIABLE

A variable is a temporary storage unit in which a value can be stored for a certain amount of time. The data-type of the variable has to be declared whenever a variable is planned for use.

There are many ways of allocating a value to a variable. In this chapter, let us look at some of the ways of allocating value to a variable.

INITIALIZATION OF A VARIABLE

When a variable is declared for use, the first value that is assigned in it is called the initial value of the variable. The process of assigning the initial value in a variable is called initialization of a variable.

For example, assume a variable (fm) that will store the full marks of an examination. A general starting value of this variable is 100. Hence, we can say that – initialize the variable fm to 100.

Syntax : int fm = 100 ;

For other general cases, variables are initialized to 0. double d = 0.0 ;

In some exceptional cases,variables are initialized to some other specific values.

Note :

Initialization is a special case of assignment.

PARAMETER OR ARGUMENT

In a variable, value can be allotted by sending it as an argument through the parameter list of the method. The parameter list is present along with the method name.

It has been shown below in the example. In the method, fnAdd() , there are two parameters(a, b) whose values are sent through the input box.

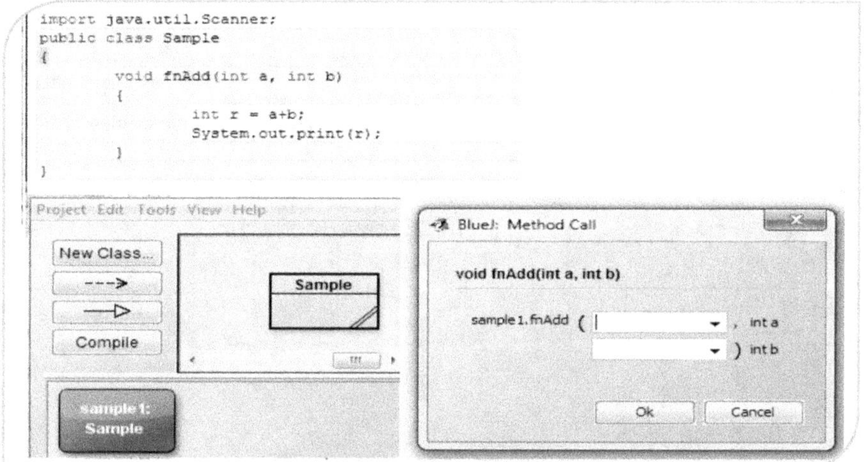

PACKAGES

A package is a collection of related classes, which have pre-defined methods, variables and interfaces that a programmer can use in his/her application. The classes of a package contain built-in methods that can be readily used by the programmer.

When we use built-in library methods in a program, we need to specify the name of the class or package which contains that method.

For example, for performing input/output operations, **java.io** package contains built in methods. For accessing standard utility methods, **java.util** package can be used.

To access all the classes of a package, operator * can be used, as shown import java.util.* ;

To access any specific class of a package, the class name has to be specified, as shown import java.util.Scanner ;

Java contains many packages which in turn contain many library classes. Some of the frequent packages and their commonly used members are given below:

java.io : It contains members that help in system input and output.

- **BufferedReader**
- **BufferedWriter**
- **DataInputStream**
- **DataOutputStream**
- **IOException**

java.lang : It contains members that are fundamental to the design of the Java programming language. This package is automatically imported in Java program.

Wrapper classes (such as Integer, Boolean), String, Math, System (standard input | output).

- **ArrayIndexOutOfBoundsException**
- **NullPointerException**

java.util : It contains some utility members such as

- **StringTokenizer**
- **Scanner**
- **Calendar**
- **Date**

Java is a friendly language and permits to **create our own packages** that we can use in programming.

Syntax of user defined package:

The syntax is : package <package-name>;

For example:

```
package school;
class teacher
{
    //code
}

class student
{
    //code
}
```

As we know, a package is a collection of classes, therefore, all defined classes like teacher and student are the members of the created package named school. [More details, explained later]

INPUT/OUTPUT

Stream

A stream can be defined as a sequence of data. There are two kinds of Streams :

- InputStream – The InputStream is used to read data from a source.

- OutputStream – The OutputStream is used for writing data to a destination.

Standard I/O Streams

Like other programming languages, Java too provide support for standard Input / Output by allowing the user's program to take input from a keyboard and produce an output on the computer screen. Java provides the following three standard streams:

- **Standard Input :** It is an *InputStream,* used to feed the data to user's program and usually a keyboard is used as standard input stream and represented as *System. in.*

- **Standard Output :** It is a *PrintStream,* used to output the data produced by the user's program and usually a computer screen is used for standard output stream and represented as *System.out.*

- **Standard Error :** This is used to output the error data produced by the user's program and usually a computer screen is used for standard error stream and represented as *System.err.* This will show the errors in red text on the screen.

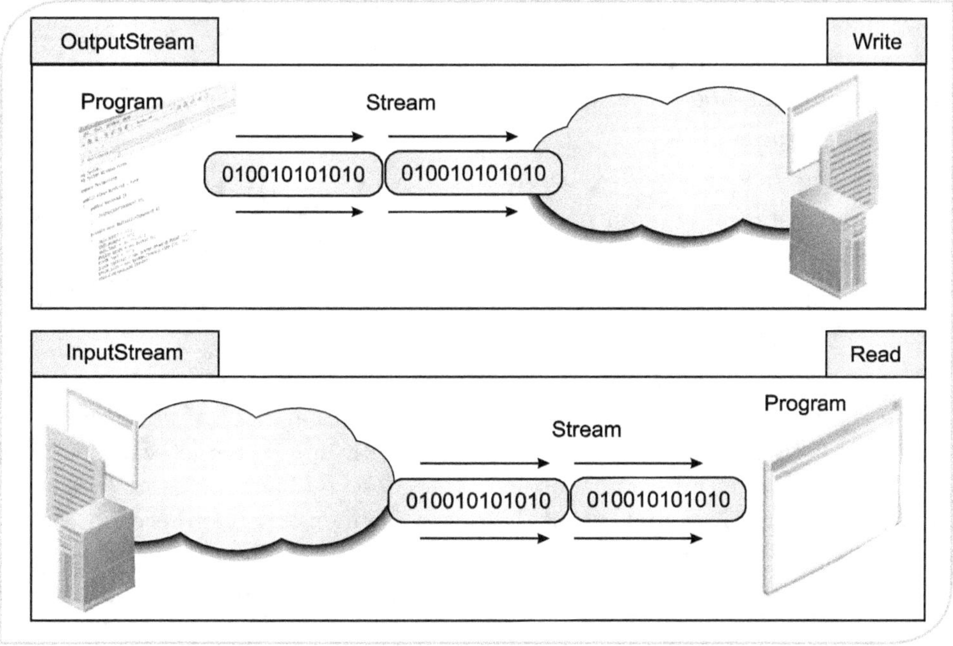

I/O Stream

Input Statements

In this section, let us see one of the ways to take input for variables of various types such as integer, double, char, string, boolean etc. there are many ways like **Using the BufferedReader** class, **Using Scanner class**. Both BufferedReader and Scanner can read a file or user input from command prompt in Java.

Two major differences between **Buffered Reader class** and **Scanner class** are:

(i) BufferedReader has significantly larger buffer memory than Scanner. Use BufferedReader if you want to get long strings from a stream, and use Scanner if you want to parse specific type of token from a stream.

(ii) BufferedReader *can only read* String but Scanner can read both String and other data types like int, float, long, double, float etc.

1. Using the BufferedReader class

Some methods automatically throw an exception, especially BufferedReader classes. Therefore we use 'throws IOException' with the method.

With a try..catch block, the error generated can be caught at the point of occurrence and can be handled by the programmer in his/her own way.

Observe the Program Code

```
BufferedReader reader = new BufferedReader(new InputStreamReader(System.in));
System.out.print("Enter your name: ");
String name = reader.readLine();
System.out.print("Good Morning  " + name);
```

In the above example, the readLine() method reads a line of text entered by the user from the command line, stores the value in the variable "name" and displays the value as stated in the System.out.println method.

2. Using Scanner class

```
Scanner obj = new Scanner(System.in);
System.out.print("Enter your name: ");
String name = obj.nextLine();
System.out.print("Enter your age: ");
int age = obj.nextInt();
System.out.print("Your name is " + name + " and your age is "+age);
```


In the above line of code, obj is an object of the Scanner class, and the statement obj. next line(), reads from the console and stores the user input in "name" variable, similarly obj.nextInt() reads the input from console in Integer format and stores in "age" variable. System.out.print() displays the output. Like this scanner class can be used for various types of data *e.g.* float, char etc..

The Scanner class can be used for various types of data input, e.g. float, char etc..

Some commonly used methods of Scanner class for taking input are :

Method detail	Program Syntax
int nextShort()	This method returns the short data type which corresponds to the short token on the Scanner buffer. Scanner sc = new Scanner (System.in); int d = sc.nextShort();
int nextInt()	Returns an integer int d = sc.nextInt();
int nextDouble ()	Returns a double double db = sc.nextDouble ();

int nextFloat ()	Returns the next floating (number) float ft = sc.nextFloat ();
int nextLong()	Returns the next token as a long. long db = sc.nextLong ();
int next()	Returns the next word String sw = sc.next();
int nextLine()	Returns the next sentence String st = sc.nextLine();
char next.charAt(0)	Returns the character System.out.print ("Enter a character : "); char c = obj.next().charAt(0);

Errors in a Program

Errors in a program can cause wrong output. There are three types of errors that can take place in a program – Syntax, Logical, Runtime.

Syntax Error : During compilation, a Syntax Error is reported by the compiler if the program is not written as per specification. They are easier to detect with the help of the compiler.

For example, r = a ? b;   reason ? is not an operator.

Java compiler has a list of syntax error messages that are helpful for understanding the error.

Shown below are some of the **most common syntax errors**

- Wrong spelling of keywords
- Missing terminator (; semicolon) or wrong punctuation mark
- Missing or mismatching brackets ( ) or { }
- Data type mismatch
- Forgetting to import a package

Logical Error : This kind of error occurs when the logic of the program is not correct. The compiler cannot detect logical errors. The programmer must analyze the program very carefully to detect a logical errors.

For example, symbol + being used for multiplication.

Shown below are some of the **most common logical errors :**

- Incorrect operator,
  For example : + instead of *
- Absence of brackets in mathematical expressions when necessary,
  For example : (a+b)/ (a – b) is not same as   a + b / a – b
- Mismatching brackets in mathematical expressions,
  For example : (a+b / a) – b is not same as   (a + b) / a - b
- Wrong initialization of a variable,
  For example : If a counter is initialized to 1 instead of 0, the result will be erroneous.

- Incorrect limits in a loop causing it to be an infinite loop,

  For example : for (int k = 15; k>10 ; k++) is an infinite loop

Runtime Error : This kind of error occurs at run time when the choice of variables gives infinite values as a result.

For example, r = a/b is a normal calculation but will cause a runtime error if variable b becomes 0.

Runtime error also occurs if the computer faces shortage of memory or other hardware problems.

COMMENTS

Comments are those parts of a program that do not get executed. They explain the working of a code in simple language. There are many uses of writing comments in a program, few of them are listed below :

- understanding a program in a better way
- debugging in case of errors
- making code maintenance easier
- making your code understandable to others in case of a team working on any project

In Java, comments are of **three types**: Single Line, Multiple Line, and Documentation

Single line comment – It ignores the part of the line that comes after it. It begins with //

Example : // a single line comment

Multiple line comment : It ignores the part that is enclosed within it. It begins with /* and ends with */

Example :

/* a multiple

line comment */

Documentation Comment : It encloses documentation on the program or any method. It begins with /** and ends with */

Example :

/**   documentation

...

...

...   */

Let's look at an example :

```java
import java.io.*;
public class SampleInput1
{
    public void main() throws IOException
    {
        // Comment 1 - declaring variables and initializing them
        int r=0; double d = 0.0; String s = ""; char c = ' '; boolean b = false;
        //Comment 2 - creating BufferedReader object for taking input
```

BufferedReader buf = new BufferedReader (new InputStreamReader (System. in));

//**Comment 3** - prompting the user to input different types of data
System.out.print(" Enter the integer number : ");
r = Integer.parseInt(buf.readLine());
System.out.print(" Enter the double number : ");
d = Double.parseDouble(buf.readLine());
System.out.print(" Enter the string (in one line) : ");
s = buf.readLine();
System.out.print(" Enter the boolean value : ");
b = Boolean.parseBoolean(buf.readLine());
System.out.print(" Enter the character : ");
c = (char) buf.read();
//**Comment 4** - Printing the data with the data type
System.out.println(" The integer is : " + r + " \n The double is : " + d);
System.out.println(" The string is : " + s + "   \n The boolean is : " + b);
System.out.println(" The character is : " + c);

}

}

MATHEMATICAL LIBRARY METHODS

pow(x,y),   sqrt(x),   cbrt(x),   ceil(x),   floor(x),   abs(x),
max(a, b),   min(a, b),   random()

Math class is present under package java.lang.

The following table shows the detail of certain Mathematic and Logical methods.

Method Detail	Program Syntax
double pow(double x, double y)	double yy = Math.pow(p, q); It returns the value of a variable to the power of another. If p = 4, q = 2 then yy = 16.0
double sqrt(double a)	double sq = Math.sqrt(x); It returns the positive square root of a number. If x = 36 , then sq = 6.0
double cbrt(double a)	double cb = Math.cbrt(x); It returns the positive cubic root of a number. If x = 42.875 , then cb = 3.5
double ceil(double a)	double cl = Math.ceil(x); It returns the nearest next integer value. If x = 62.8 , then cl = 63 If x − 47.3 , then cl = 48

double floor(double a)	double fl = Math.floor(x); It returns the nearest previous integer value. If x = 24.9 , then fl = 24 If x = 36.3 , then fl = 36
double round(x)	double fl = Math.round (x); It returns the nearest integer value. If x = 14.6 , then fl = 15 If x = 92.7 , then fl = 93
int abs(int a)	int ab = Math.abs(p); It returns the absolute value of the argument, which is the value without the sign. If p = 17 , then ab = 17 If p = -6 , then ab = 6
int max(int a, int b)	int gt = Math.max(p, q); It returns the larger of the two arguments which should be of the same data-type as that of the return. max( ) is an overloaded function which works for data types int/long/float/double as well. If p = 15, q = 19 then gt = 19 If p = 331.6, q = 331.4 then gt = 331.6 , here p, q, gt are double
int min(int a, int b)	int st = Math.min(p1, q1); It returns the smaller of the two arguments which should be of the same data-type as that of the return min ( ) is an overloaded function which works for data types int/long/float/double as well. If p = 15, q = 19 then st = 15 If p = 331.6, q = 331.4 then st = 331.4 , here p, q, st are double
double random()	double rn = Math.random(); It returns a positive random number lying between 0.0 and 1.0 Whenever this statement is executed, a random number is placed in rn.

JAVA EXPRESSION : USING ALL THE OPERATORS AND METHODS OF MATH CLASS

A Java expression is a sequence of values, variables, operators and methods that perform calculation and return some result.

They form an integral part of a program as an expression is needed for performing any calculation.

In this section, we will look at the application of expressions in a program and how to convert mathematical expressions into Java program expressions.

Convert the given mathematical expressions to Java program expressions

1. Mathematical Expression : $r = (a + b) \div c$

   Java Program Expression : r = (a + b) / c

2. Mathematical Expression : $p = \dfrac{m + n}{m^2 + h^4}$

   Java Program Expression : p = (m + n) / (m*m + Math.pow (h, 4))

3. Mathematical Expression : $w = m^p + n^q$;

   Java Program Expression : w = Math.pow(m,p) + Math.pow(n, q)

4. Mathematical Expression : $p = 5.125 - \dfrac{3y^2}{2 + y}$

   Java Program Expression : p =5.125 – (3 * (y * y) /(2 + y))

5. Mathematical Expression : $d = (7a^4 * 2b) / (a^2 + b^2)$

   Java Program Expression : d = (7 * Math.pow(a ,4) * 2 * b) / (a*a + b*b)

6. Mathematical Expression : $d = (a+b)\, n \div (\sqrt{3} + b)$

   Java Program Expression : d = (a + b) * n / (Math.sqrt(3) + b)

7. Mathematical Expression : $g = (p^5 - m^4)/ r^2 * \sqrt{(q + b)}$

   Java Program Expression : g = (Math.pow(p, 5) – Math.pow(m, 4))/(r*r) * Math.
   sqrt(q + b)

8. Mathematical Expression: $h = a + \dfrac{b^2\ \ c^3}{d^y * e^5}$

   Java Program Expression : h = a+(b*b – Math.pow(c,3))/(Math.pow(d,4) * Math.
   pow(e,5))

9. Mathematical Expression: $k = 12\,y^2 + 24g^4 / 48h^6$

   Java Program Expression: k = 12*y*y + 24 * Math.pow(g, 4)/ 48 * Math.pow
   (h, 6)

10. Mathematical Expression : $m = \dfrac{a}{b^3} + \dfrac{c}{d^5}\ \ \dfrac{e}{f^9}$

    Java Program Expression : m = a/Math.pow(b,3) + c/Math.pow(d,5) + e/ Math.
    pow(f,9)

SUMMARY

- A variable is a temporary storage unit in which a value can be stored for a certain amount of time.
- The first value that is assigned in a variable is called its initial value.
- A package in Java is a collection of classes that can be imported in a program. The classes of a package contain built-in methods that can be used in a program.
- Java provides the following three standard I/O streams :
  - **Standard Input :** It is used to feed the data to user's program and usually a keyboard is used as standard input stream and represented as System.in.
  - **Standard Output :** It is used to output the data produced by the user's program and usually a computer screen is used for standard output stream and represented as System.out.
  - **Standard Error :** This is used to output the error data produced by the user's program and usually a computer screen is used for standard error stream and represented as System.err.
- Scanner Class contains classes that help in taking input from the standard input stream.
- There are three types of errors that can take place in a program :

  Syntax Error : It is reported by the compiler if the program is not written as per specification.

  Logical Error : It occurs when the logic of the program is not correct. It cannot be reported by the compiler.

  Runtime Error : This kind of error occurs at run time when the choice of variables gives infinite values as a result.
- Commenting involves placing Human readable description inside of computer programs detailing what the code is doing.
- Comments are those parts of a program that do not get executed. Java comments are of **three types**: Single Line, Multiple Line, Documentation

  ```
  // a single line comment
  /* a multiple
     line comment */
  /** documentation
  ...
  ...
  ... */
  ```
- Math class is present under package java.lang.
- Mathematical Methods are given by Java for our help. Some important methods are
  - **Math.pow(p, q) :** to calculate the value of **p** to the power of **q** (p^q)
  - **Math.sqrt(p) :**   to calculate the value of square root of argument **p**
  - **Math.cbrt(p) :**   to calculate the value of cubic root of argument **p**
  - **Math.max(p, q) :** to return the maximum of arguments **p , q**
  - **Math.min(p, q) :** to return the minimum of arguments **p , q**

SOLVED QUESTIONS

1. **What are the types of errors that can take place in a program? Explain in brief.**

   Answer : There are three types of errors that can take place in a program – Syntax, Logical, Runtime.

   Syntax Error : During compilation, a Syntax Error is reported by the compiler if the program is not written as per specification. They are easier to detect with the help of the compiler. For example r = a x b; Reason x is not an operator.

   Logical Error : This kind of error occurs when the logic of the program is not correct. For example + symbol is used for multiplication. The compiler cannot detect logical error and so need more care to be detected.

   Runtime Error : This kind of error occurs at run time when the choice of variables gives infinite values as a result. For example r = a/b is a normal calculation but will cause a runtime error if variable b becomes 0.

2. **Which of the following are valid comments ?**

   (i)   /* comment */

   (ii)   /* comment

   (iii) // comment

   (iv) */ comment */

   Answer : (i) /*comment */ & (iii) //comment are valid comments.

3. **Give the output of the following math functions :**

   (i) Math.ceil(4.2)   (ii) Math.abs(– 4)

   Answer : (i) 5.0, (ii) 4

4. **What are the values stored in variables r1 and r2 ?**

   (i) double r1 = Math.abs(Math.min(–2.83,–5.83));

   (ii) double r2 = Math.sqrt(Math.floor) 16.3));

   Answer : r1 = 5.83

   r2 = 4.0

5. **What will the following functions return when executed ?**

   (i) Math.max(-17, - 19)   (ii) Math.ceil(7.8)

   Answer. (i) –17   (ii) 8

EXERCISE

Question 1 : Answer the following in brief :

(a) Which keyword is used to access members of another package ?

(b) What does a package contain ?

Question 2 : Name the package of the following :

(a) Scanner   (b) Math   (c) Calendar

(d) BufferedReader   (e) StringTokenizer

Question 3 : Write the difference between the following and give example :

(a) Syntax Error & Logical Error

(b) Math.pow(p,q) & Math.sqrt(p,q)

Question 4 : Write the output of the codes given below :

(a) double df = Math.floor (23.35); double dc = Math.ceil (23.35);

System.out.print(" DF = " + df + " DC = " + dc);

(b) double pa = 25.0 , pb = 0.6;

double pr = Math.sqrt (pa) - Math.pow (pb, 2);

System.out.println("Ans : " + pr);

(c) double dc = -62.4 ; double de = Math.ceil (Math.abs(dc));

System.out.println (" DE = " + de);

(d) int ab = 948 ; int a = Math.max (ab%100 , ab/100);

System.out.println(" A = " + a);

(e) int y = 72, a = 27 , r = 10 ;

r = r + (y+a) % a

System.out.println(" R = " + r);

Question 5 : Write one line program code for the following situations :

1   A farmer wants to feed his cows with grass, he has a total 230 gms of grass and each cow takes at least 15 gms of grass each day, then write a program to calculate the number of cows he can feed, remember number of cows can't be in fraction.

2. Imagine on your birthday your parents have given you a total of ₹ 250/- and you have decided to give your friends a return gift of a pencil bag where each pencil bag costs ₹ 15/-. Hence write a program to calculate the number of friends you can invite in your birthday? Remember you can't invite a "half friend".

3. Write the program to calculate the square root of 12.25.

4. If the cube of a number is 3.375 then write a program to find the number.

5. Let's say A=14 and B=25, write a program to calculate the difference between A and B.

6. What would be the next upper value of 22.45 and 27.55 ?

7. If you ride a taxi and if the fare after reaching your destination is ₹ 138.65 then write a program to calculate the fare which you should pay in cash ?

8. Round off these values to their nearest integer by using functions of java ?
(i) 25.87   (ii) 89.25   (iii) 117.98

9. Write a program to calculate the value of R without using the multiplication operator, where   R = 5 * 5 * 5 * 5

10. What will be the final value in T where T = Math.max(Math.min (757, 759) , Math.pow(25,2));

Chapter 5

CONDITIONAL CONSTRUCTS IN JAVA

Contents

- Introduction
  - ❖ Relational Operators
  - ❖ Logical Operators
- Programming Constructs
  - ❖ Sequence Construct
  - ❖ Conditional Construct
  - ❖ Iteration Construct
- Conditional Statements in Java
  - ❖ if ... else
    - ◆ if
    - ◆ if..else
    - ◆ Condition Ladder
    - ◆ Nested if....else
  - ❖ Switch .... Case
    - ◆ Use of default in Switch Case
    - ◆ Fall Through in Switch Case
  - ❖ Comparison of if...else and switch ... case statements
  - ❖ Ternary Operator
- Menu Driven Program
  - ❖ System exit (0)
- Solved Programs
  - ❖ On if ... else conditional,
  - ❖ On switch...case
  - ❖ On ternary Operator
- Summary
- Solved questions
- Exercise

INTRODUCTION

We come across various conditions in our daily life. Most of the works that we do are dependent on some or the other conditions. For example, carry the umbrella if it is a rainy season or set the alarm if you have to get up early.

A conditional work is done only if the condition is true. In case a condition is false, either do nothing or do something else. For example, if you are in a hurry, go by a taxi otherwise go by a bus.

In Java, we can implement conditions using certain tools. In the coming sections, we will learn how to apply conditions in a Java program but for this first, we must understand about the operators. Java provides different types of operators [*Refer previous chapter Introduction to Java-Data Values and Types*] but for conditions, we mainly use two types of operators :

Relational Operators

These operators help in creating a condition. They are mainly used for the comparison of variables. Java has six relational operators, shown in the following table :

Operator	Use	Operator	Use
>	Greater than	<=	Less than or equal to
<	Less than	==	Comparison of Equality
>=	Greater Than or Equal to	!=	Comparison of Inequality

Observe the following conditions and fill in the blanks :

(i)   Q = 25; T = 55   (Q == T) will be _________ (True/False)

(ii) Q = 25; T = 55 ; R = Q*2;   (R >= T) will be _________ (True/False)

(iii) Q = 25; T = 55; W = Q+30   (Q != T) will be _________ (True/False)

Logical Operators

These operators help to connect more than one condition. Java has three logical operators :

Operator	Use	Result
!	NOT	Reverses the result of a given condition
&&	AND	Result is True only if all the conditions are True
||	OR	Result is True if any one of the conditions is True

A condition may be single or composite. A composite condition is made up of multiple conditions which are connected by using logical operators (AND and OR).

Observe the following conditions and fill in the blanks :

(i)   Q = 25; T = 55; (Q> 20 && T<100) will be .... (True/False)

(ii) Q = 25; T = 55 ; R = Q*2; (R == 75 || Q<T) will be .... (True/False)

(iii) Q = 25; T = 55; V = Q – T (Q !=20 && V<= (T-25)) will be ....(True/False)

PROGRAMMING CONSTRUCTS

In a program, the statements are categorized into specific constructs
- Sequence Construct
- Conditional Construct
- Iteration Construct

The statements in a program are executed in a specific order depending upon the construct they fall under.

Sequence Construct

It is the category in which the statements are executed one after another in a sequence.

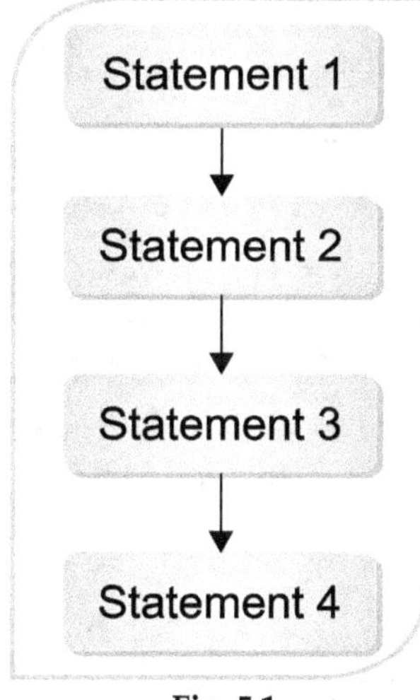

Fig. 5.1

Conditional Construct

It is the category in which the statements are executed only if they satisfy a given condition.

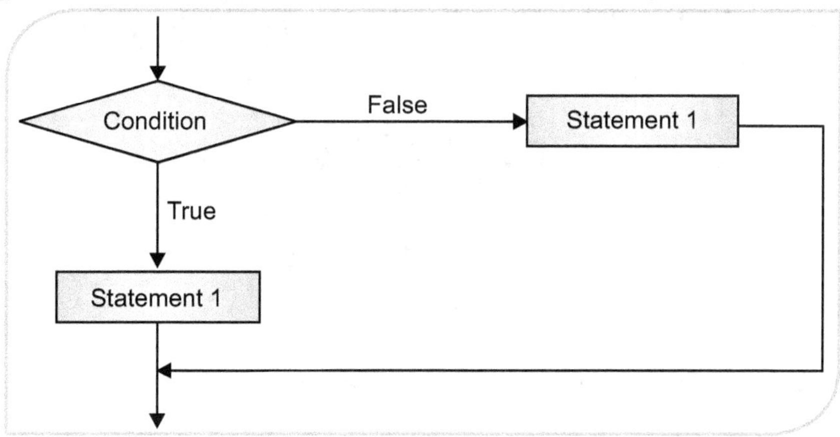

Fig. 5.2

Iteration Construct

It is the category in which a group of statements are executed repeatedly as long as a given condition is true.

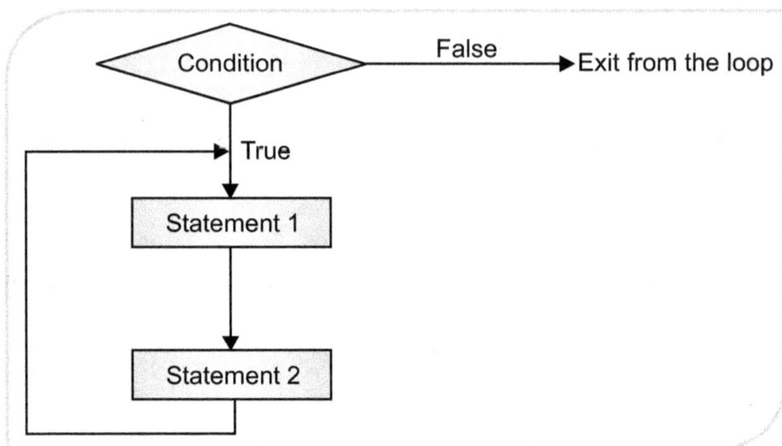

Fig. 5.3

CONDITIONAL STATEMENTS IN JAVA

A condition is a statement that has a choice of result of either True or False. The flow of a single conditional statement is as follows :

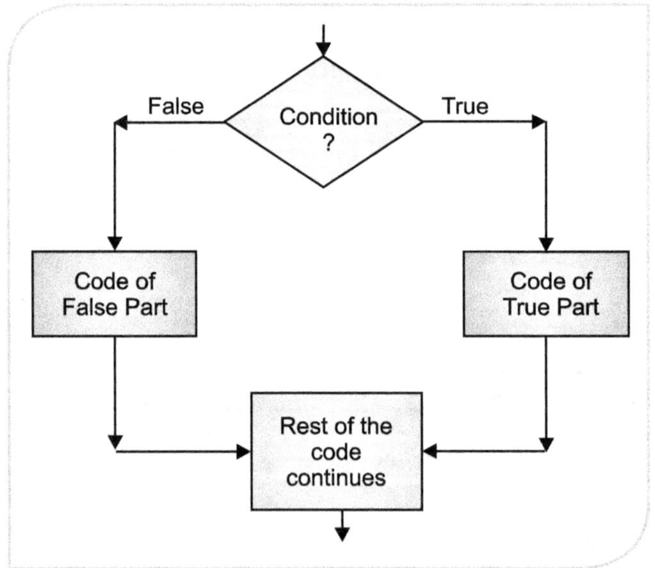

Fig. 5.4

Note :

Code can be a single statement or a group of statements.

The flow of a multiple conditional statement is as follows :

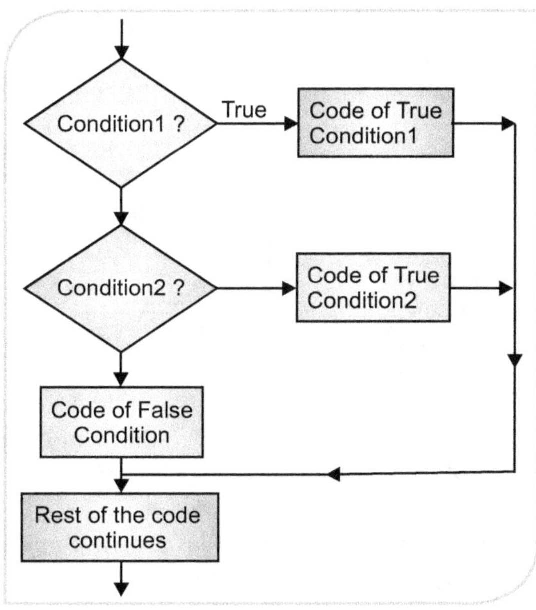

Fig. 5.5

Java has three Conditional Statements :

(i)   if...else

(ii) switch...case

(iii) ternary operator

if ... else

It is a conditional statement that creates separate paths in the program flow of statements. It takes a condition which has two divisions, true part and false part. If the condition is true, then the true part gets executed and if the condition is false, then the false part gets executed. Both the true and the false part can never get executed together.

Conditional statement if...else is used mainly in cases where a condition decides what will be the next course of action. For example, to verify whether a number is even or odd, a number is prime or not, etc.

This conditional statement can be implemented in four forms, as shown below :

<table>
<tr><td>

(i) Only one condition

```
if (condition)
{
     Block of statements
}
```

</td><td>

(ii) A condition with true and false

```
if (condition1)
{
     Block of statements 1
}
else
{
     Block of statements 2
}
```

</td></tr>
</table>

<table>
<tr><td>

(iii) condition ladder

```
if (condition1)
{
    Block of statements 1
}
else if(condition2)
{
    Block of statements 2
}
else if(condition3)
{
    Block of statements 3
}
else
{
    Final Block of statements
}
```

</td><td>

(iv) Nested 'ifs'

```
if (condition1)
{
    if (condition2)
    {
        Block of statements 1
    }
    else
    {
        Block of statements 2
    }
}
else
{
    Block of statements 3
}
```

</td></tr>
</table>

In case of **only one condition**, if the condition is true then the statements under it get executed. If it is false, then nothing happens.

In case of **a condition with true and false**, if the condition is true then the statements under it get executed and if it is not true, then the statements under else get executed.

In case of **condition ladder**, there is more than one condition connected to each other. They are verified one after another. Whenever any condition becomes true, statements under it get executed and the rest of the conditions are not even verified. The control comes out of the conditional block.

In case of **Nested 'ifs' Condition,** It has conditions laid out in such a manner that one condition if true, leads to another condition.

If condition1 is true, then further if condition2 is true then 'Block of statements 1' get executed else 'Block of statements 2' get executed. If condition1 is false then 'Block of statements 3' get executed. Nested conditions can be placed inside the 'if' part or inside the 'else' part or inside the 'if' and 'else' both parts.

Examples of if...else Statement

Assume that an item has some sellprice and costprice at any point of time. Then depending upon the value of these variables, print statement will get executed.

```
if ( sellprice>costprice )
{
    System.out.print( " Profit " );
}
else
{
System.out.print( " Loss " );
}
```

Assume another example, to print the number of digits present in a number, say n, using its values. In the code shown below, if any one condition becomes true, then the other conditions will not be tested and the control will come out of the block.

The code depends upon the value of **n** at any given point of time. Variable **n** can assume different values at different points of time.

```
if ( n <10 )
{
    System.out.print( "One Digit Number " );
}
elseif ( n <100 )
{
    System.out.print( "Two Digit Number " );
}
elseif ( n <1000 )
{
    System.out.print( "Three Digit Number " );
}
elseif ( n <10000 )
{
    System.out.print( "Four Digit Number " );
}
else
{
System.out.print( "Very Big Number" );
}
```

Switch...Case

There are many conditional statements which involve only the comparison of equality. For example, choice of floor number in a lift of multistoried building or the choice of code number in case of a product. In these kind of cases, switch...case conditional statement is appropriate.

This conditional statement is used in cases where the comparison is of equality only.

The syntax is shown below :

```
switch (expression)
{
    case value 1 :   block of code 1
                     break;
    case value 2 :   block of code 2
                     break;
    case value 3 :   block of code 3
                     break;
    default      :   final block of code
}
```

Simple Example :

Assume that P indicates the points scored in an exam. Depending upon the value of P, the following code prints in how many subjects the score was more than 80%.

```
switch (P)
{
    case 5 :  System.out.print ( "Scored more than 80% in Five subjects." );
              break;
    case 4 :  System.out.print ( "Scored more than 80% in Four subjects." );
              break;
    case 3 :  System.out.print ( "Scored more than 80% in Three subjects." );
              break;
    case 2 :  System.out.print ( "Scored more than 80% in Two subjects." );
              break;
    case 1 :  System.out.print ( "Scored more than 80% in One subject." );
              break;
    default : System.out.print ( "Sorry, No points." );
}
```

Use of 'default' in Switch... Case

In Switch Case statement, default becomes active when none of the cases match. Default and the block present under it should appear at last.

Default in Switch...Case is optional. Without its presence, there will be no action in the Switch...Case block, when none of the cases will match.

Examples of Switch ...Case Statement

Example : Input two numbers and an operator choice. Perform the operations of a five function calculator. [For the operator choice, use a char type variable opch.]

```
switch (opch)
{
    case '+' :  res = an + bn;
        System.out.print("\n " + an + "  + " + bn + " = " + res);
        break;
    case '-' :  res = an - bn;
        System.out.print("\n " + an + " - " + bn + " = " + res);
        break;
    case '*' :  res = an * bn;
        System.out.print("\n " + an + " * " + bn + " = " + res);
        break;
    case '/' : res = an/bn;
        System.out.print("\n " + an + " / " + bn + " = " + res);
        break;
    case '%' : res = an % bn;
        System.out.print("\n " + an + " % " + bn + " = " + res);
        break;
    default : System.out.print("\n Operator choice " + opch + " is INVALID. ");
}
```

OUTPUT

an = 25

bn = 35

Enter the operator choice (+ - * / %) : -

 25 - 35 = -10

an = 65

bn = 50

Enter the operator choice (+ - * / %) : %

 65 % 50 = 15

an = 65

bn = 36

Enter the operator choice (+ - * / %) : &

Operator choice 8 is INVALID.

Importance of Break in Switch Case & Fall through Situation

The break statement causes the program flow to exit from the body of the switch construct. Control goes to the first statement following the end of the switch-case construct.

If break statement is not given then, all the statements that appear below the matching case, get executed. This situation is called **Fall Through.**

Example : (showing Fall Through) Input a number and print the corresponding day of the week.

```
//Weekday from day number... program showing Logical Error of Fall Through
switch (wn)
{
    case 1  : System.out.println(" wn = " + wn + "  weekday is SUNDAY.");
    case 2  : System.out.println(" wn = " + wn + " weekday is MONDAY.");
    case 3  : System.out.println(" wn = " + wn + " weekday is TUESDAY.");
    case 4  : System.out.println(" wn = " + wn + " weekday is WEDNESDAY.");
    case 5  : System.out.println(" wn = " + wn + " weekday is THURSDAY.");
    case 6  : System.out.println(" wn = " + wn + " weekday is FRIDAY.");
    case 7  : System.out.println(" wn = " + wn + " weekday is SATURDAY.");
    default : System.out.println(" wn = " + wn + " is an INVALID day number. ");
```

OUTPUT

Enter the day number : 5

wn = 5 weekday is THURSDAY.

wn = 5 weekday is FRIDAY.

wn = 5 weekday is SATURDAY.

wn = 5 is an INVALID day number.

[Reason – it enters for the matching case but goes through all the following cases

Enter the day number: 9

wn = 9 is an INVALID day number.

Observe the output of the above code for the following inputs :

(i) wn = 2   (ii) wn = 7   (iii) wn = 0

Comparison of if...else and switch...case Statements

S.N.	if ... else	switch ... case
1.	All relational operators (greater than, less than, etc) can be used.	Only comparison of equality operator is used.
2.	Two variables can be compared.	Only a variable and a constant can be compared.
3.	Multiple conditions can be connected by using logical operators.	Multiple conditions using logical operators cannot be connected.
4.	All data types are allowed.	Variables of type integer (byte, short, int, long) and char only can be used.
5.	Preferred in cases where there are conditions other than equality comparison.	Preferred in cases where there are simple conditions of equality.
6.	Gives more variety and is better for bigger and complicated situations.	Gives less variety and is better for smaller and simpler situations.
7.	No use of break. Fall through not possible but brackets must match.	Break is needed to avoid fall through.

Ternary Operator

Ternary operator is used in cases where the condition is small and true and false zones contain values to assign to result. The syntax is shown below :

Syntax : result = (condition) ?true zone : false zone ;

Examples of Ternary Operator :

(i)   min = (a < b) ? a : b;   //min gets a if a is less than b, b otherwise

(ii)   s = (y!= 0) ? (x/y) : 0;   // this allows x/y to happen only if (y != 0)

(iii) d = (a>b) ? (a-b) : (b-a) ;   // d is the difference between a, b , always positive

(iv) r = (p% q ==0) ? 1 : 0;   // r gets 1 if q is a factor of p, 0 otherwise

Note :

- Check the output with any values in the variables.

MENU DRIVEN PROGRAMS

Menu driven programs are those in which a variable is used for making a choice from a list of options. If the choice is out of the list then an error message is generated and the program terminates.

Java provides a statement **System.exit(0)** which helps in terminating a program immediately by abandoning the succeeding statements. This statement can be used to terminate a program in case of invalid choice.

Example of a Menu Driven Program :

(Create a five function calculator that performs the operations of arithmetic operators   + – * / % by applying a menu).

```java
//mini calculator with 5 operators
import java.util.*;
class ProgMenu
{
    void main( )
    {
        int fn=0, sn=0, ch = 0, res = 0 ;  Scanner sc = new Scanner (System.in );
        System.out.print("\n\n Enter the first number: "); fn = sc.nextInt();
        System.out.print(" Enter the second number: "); sn = sc.nextInt();
        System.out.println (" Make a choice from the menu given below – ");
        System.out.println (" Enter 1 for    +" );
        System.out.println (" Enter 2 for    -" );
        System.out.println (" Enter 3 for    *" );
        System.out.println (" Enter 4 for    /" );
        System.out.println (" Enter 5 for    %" );
        System.out.println (" Enter your choice : " );
        ch = sc.nextInt();
        if ( ch < 1 || ch > 5 )
        {
            System.out.print("\n Wrong choice of operator.");
            System.exit(0) ;
        }
        else if(ch == 1)
        {
            res = fn + sn;
            System.out.print("\n Sum of " + fn + " and " + sn + " = " + res  );
        }
        else if(ch == 2)
        {
            res = fn - sn;
            System.out.print("\n Difference between " + fn + " and " + sn + " = " + res  );
        }
        else if(ch == 3)
        {
            res = fn * sn;
            System.out.print("\n Product of " + fn + " and " + sn + " = " + res  );
```

```
            }
        else if(ch == 4)
        {
            res = fn / sn;
            System.out.print("\n Quotient of " + fn + " by " + sn + " = " + res  );
        }
        else if(ch == 5)
        {
            res = fn % sn;
            System.out.print("\n Remainder of " + fn + " by " + sn + " = " + res  );
        }
    }
}
```

OUTPUT

Enter the first number: 200	Enter the first number: 150
Enter the second number: 4	Enter the second number: 45
Make a choice from the menu given below–	Make a choice from the menu given below –
Enter 1 for +	Enter 1 for +
Enter 2 for -	Enter 2 for -
Enter 3 for *	Enter 3 for *
Enter 4 for /	Enter 4 for /
Enter 5 for %	Enter 5 for %
Enter your choice : 3	Enter your choice : 10
Product of 200 and 4 is 800	Invalid Choice

SOLVED PROGRAMS

On if.. else Conditional Statements

Program 1 : Input the temperature of water in a beaker. In case the temperature is equal to 100 then print "The Water is Boiling".

Program Idea :

* Input a number for temp
* Use a condition for verifying the value of temp
* The output statement in this program is conditional

`import java.util.*;`	**OUTPUT**
`class ProgA`	Temp = 100
`{`	The Water is Boiling.
`    void main()`	Temp = 90
`    {`	(no output in this case)

```
            int temp = 0;
            Scanner sc = new Scanner (System.in);
            System.out.print (" Enter temp : ");
            temp = sc.nextInt();
            if(temp == 100)
            {
                    System.out.print("\n The Water
                                        is Boiling. " );
            }
        }
    }
```

The condition in the above program can be modified so that it shows an output when the condition is false.

```
...
if(temp == 100)
{
    System.out.print("\n The Water is Boiling. " );
}
else
{
    System.out.print("\n The Water is NOT Boiling. " );
}
```

Verify the output of the program when temp = 90, 100, etc

- -

Program 2 : Input two integers p, q. Verify if q is a factor of p or not. Print messages accordingly.

Program Idea :

- Input the two numbers
- Use condition if (p%q == 0)   for verification
- Print the output statements in conditional cases

- -

	OUTPUT
`import java.util.*;`	
`class ProgB`	
`{`	Enter p : 60
`    void main()`	Enter q : 12
`    {`	
`        int p=0, q=0;`	12 is a factor of 60
`        Scanner sc = new Scanner (System.in);`	
`        System.out.println(" Enter p : ");`	Enter p : 1000
`        p = sc.nextInt();`	Enter q : 90

```
            System.out.println (" Enter q : ");
            q = sc.nextInt();                              90 is NOT a factor of 1000
            if(p%q == 0)
            {
            System.out.print(q + " is a factor of " + p );
            }
            else
            {
            System.out.print(q+"is NOT a factor of"+p);
            }
        }
    }
```

Program 3 : In an experiment, it was observed that when an object is heated, its molecular motion increases, when it is cooled, its molecular motion decreases and its molecular motion does not change otherwise.

For an object, enter the starting temperature in st and the ending temperature in et.

If et >st then print "INCREASE in Molecular Motion".

Else If et <st then print "DECREASE in Molecular Motion".

Else Print "NO Change in Molecular Motion" .

Program Idea :

- Input values of **st** and **et**.
- Each time the program is executed with a different set of values, it should print any one of the output statements.
- The output statements are conditional.

```
import java.util.*;
classProgC
{
    void main ( )
    {
        int st = 0, et = 0 ;Scanner sc = new Scanner (System.in)
        System.out.println (" Enter the Starting Temperature : ");  sc = sc.nextInt();
        System.out.println (" Enter the Ending Temperature : ");  et = sc.nextInt();
        if(et >st)
        {
            System.out.print("\n INCREASE in Molecular Motion." );
        }
        else if (et <st)
```

```
        {
            System.out.print("\n DECREASE in Molecular Motion." );
        }
        else
        {
        System.out.print("\n NO Change in Molecular Motion." );
        }
    }
}
```

OUTPUT

Enter the Starting Temperature : 45
Enter the Ending Temperature : 65
INCREASE in Molecular Motion.

Enter the Starting Temperature : 100
Enter the Ending Temperature : 50
DECREASE in Molecular Motion.

Enter the Starting Temperature : 250
Enter the Ending Temperature : 250
NO Change in Molecular Motion.

Practice Program : *In a fabric color box, colors were coded as per Rainbow colors. On the color box, the color codes were given as follows :*

(1) Violet   (2) Indigo   (3) Blue   (4) Green   (5) Yellow   (6) Orange
(7) Red

Enter the color code in variable cd. Print the color it represents. In case the code did not match with the given choice, print "No Such color in the box".

Program Idea :

* *The program has 7 conditions to test depending on the value of the input.*

Program 4 : Enter the cost price and selling price of an item. Print whether it incurred profit or loss. Also print the profit or loss percentage, whichever applicable.

```
//to check whether an item incurred Profit or loss
import java.util.*;
class ProgE
{
    void main( )
    {
        int cp = 0, sp = 0;
        Scanner sc = new Scanner (System.in );
        System.out.print("\n Enter the cost price : ");
        cp = sc.nextInt();
        System.out.print("\n Enter the selling price : ");
```

```java
        sp =   sc.nextInt();
        if(sp>cp)
        {
            System.out.print("\n The item incurred PROFIT.");
            int pf = sp - cp;
            double pfpt = (pf * 100.0)/cp;
            System.out.print("\n The Profit Percentage = " + pfpt );
        }
        else if(sp<cp)
        {
            System.out.print("\n The item incurred LOSS.");
            int ls = cp - sp;
            double lspt = (ls * 100.0)/cp;
            System.out.print("\n The Loss Percentage = " + lspt );
        }
        else
        {
            System.out.print("\n No, The item incurred Neither PROFIT Nor LOSS.");
        }
    }
}
```

OUTPUT

Enter the cost price : 125
Enter the sell price : 150

The item incurred PROFIT.
The Profit Percentage = 20.0

Enter the cost price : 85
Enter the sell price : 25
The item incurred LOSS.
The Loss Percentage = 70.58823529411765

Enter the cost price : 100
Enter the sell price : 100
No, The item incurred Neither PROFIT Nor LOSS.

Program 5 : Create a 5 function calculator that performs the operations of arithmetic operators + – * / % by applying a menu : Validate the denominator before performing division and modulus operation.

```java
    //mini calculator with 5 operators
    import java.util.*;
    class ProgF
    {
```

```java
void main( )
{
    int fn=0, sn=0, ch = 0, res = 0 ;
    Scanner sc = new Scanner (System.in ) ;
    System.out.print("\n\n Enter the first number: ");
    fn = sc.nextInt();
    System.out.println(" Enter the second number: ");
    sn = sc.nextInt();
    System.out.print("\n Enter the desired operator [1 for +  2 for -  3 for *  4 for /  5
                                                       for %] : ");
    ch = sc.nextInt();
    if(ch == 1)
    {
        res = fn + sn;
        System.out.print("\n Sum of " + fn + " and " + sn + " = " + res  );
    }
    else if(ch == 2)
    {
        res = fn - sn;
        System.out.print("\n Difference between " + fn + " and " + sn + " = " + res  );
    }
    else if(ch == 3)
    {
        res = fn * sn;
        System.out.print("\n Product of " + fn + " and " + sn + " = " + res  );
    }
    else if(ch == 4)
    {
        if(sn != 0)
        {
            res = fn / sn;
            System.out.print("\n Quotient of " + fn + " by " + sn + " = " + res  );
        }
        else
        {
            System.out.print("\n Division by Zero not allowed. ");
        }
    }
    else if(ch == 5)
    {
        if(sn != 0)
        {
            res = fn % sn;
            System.out.print("\n Remainder of " + fn + " by " + sn + " = " + res  );
        }
```

```
            else
            {
                System.out.print("\n Error in division. ");
            }
        }
        else
        {
                System.out.print("\n Wrong choice of operator.");
        }
    }
}
```

OUTPUT

Enter the first number: 75

Enter the second number: 25

Enter the desired operator [1 for +   2 for - 3 for *   4 for /   5 for %]: 1

Sum of 75 and 25 = 100

Enter the first number: 75

Enter the second number: 25

Enter the desired operator [1 +   2 - 3 *   4 /   5 %] : 2

Difference between 75 and 25 = 50

Program 6 : Calculate the value of T, by taking input of R , K & S , given that

$$T = R^2 + K^3 \qquad \text{when } S<=10$$
$$= R^3 + K^2 \qquad \text{when } S<=20 \text{ but } >10$$
$$= (R + K)^2 \qquad \text{otherwise}$$

```
//Conditional calculation of T using R, K, S
import java.util.*;
class ProgJ
{
    void main()
    {
        int S = 0, R = 0, K = 0 , T = 0;
        Scanner sc = new Scanner(System.in);
        System.out.print("\n Enter the value of S : ");
        S = sc.nextInt() ;
        System.out.print("\n Enter the value of R : ");
        R = sc.nextInt() ;
        System.out.print("\n Enter the value of K : ");
        K = sc.nextInt() ;
        f(S<= 10)
```

```java
    {
        T = R*R + K*K*K ;
    }
    else if (S < = 20 && S > 10)
    {
        T = R*R*R + K * K ;
    }
    else
    {
        T = (R+K) * (R+K) ;
    }
        System.out.print("\n The calculated result of T = " + T );
    }
}
```

Note 1 :

Calculation of T is conditional. Printing of T is common in all the cases. Therefore, the print statement to print the result is written out of the condition.

Note 2 :

In this program there is no invalid value of S.

OUTPUT

Enter the value of S: 4

Enter the value of R: 4

Enter the value of K: 3

The calculated result of T = 43

Program 7 : Input the length of the three sides of a valid triangle in s1, s2, s3. Verify whether the triangle is Equilateral or Isosceles or Scalene.

[Equilateral Triangle has length of all three sides equal, Isosceles Triangle has length of any two sides equal. Scalene Triangle has all sides unequal.]

```java
import java. util.*;
class ProgG
{
    void main()
    {
        double s1 = 0, s2 = 0, s3 = 0 ;  Scanner sc = new Scanner (System.in) ;
        System.out.println("Enter length of side 1 : ");  s1 = sc.nextDouble();
        System.out.println("Enter length of side 2 : ");  s2 = sc.nextDouble();
        System.out.println("Enter length of side 3 : ");  s3 = sc.nextDouble();
        if( s1 == s2 && s2 == s3)
        {
```

```java
            System.out.print("The Triangle is Equilateral");
        }
        else if( s1 != s2 && s2 != s3 && s1 != s3)
        {
            System.out.print("The Triangle is Scalene");
        }
        else
        {
            System.out.print("The Triangle is Isosceles");
        }
    }
}
```

OUTPUT

Enter length of side 1 : 10
Enter length of side 2 : 15
Enter length of side 3 : 10
The Triangle is Isosceles

Program 8 : A number is called RiWi Number if last two digits are same. Input a number and verify whether it is a RiWi number or not.

```java
import java.util.*;
class ProgG
{
    void main()
    {
        int n = 0, d1 = 0, d2 =0 , cn = 0 ;  Scanner sc = new Scanner (System.in) ;
        System.out.println("Enter the number  : ");  n = sc.nextInt ();
        cn = n;
        d1 = cn%10;
        cn = cn/10;
        d2 = cn % 10;
        if( d1 == d2 )
        {
            System.out.print("The Number " + n +  " is a RiWi Number");
        }
        else
        {
            System.out.print("The Number " + n +  " is NOT a RiWi Number");
        }
    }
}
```

OUTPUT

Enter the number : 7244

The Number 7244 is a RiWi Number

Enter the number : 35412

The Number 35412 is NOT a RiWi Number

On switch...case Conditional Statements

Program 9 : Input the age of a person (say g). If the age is equal to 13, print "You are Welcome to Teen club". If the age is equal to 60, print "You are Welcome to Senior Citizen Club". If none is true, print "You are Welcome as a guest".

```java
import java.util.*;
class Program
{
    void main()
    {
        int g = 0;  Scanner sc = new Scanner (System.in);
        System.out.print("\n Enter your age: ");    g = sc.nextInt();
        switch (g)
        {
            case 13 : System.out.println(" You are Welcome to Teen Club ");
                    break;
            case 60 : System.out.println(" You are Welcome to Senior Citizen Club ");
                    break;
            default :  System.out.println(" You are Welcome as a guest ");
        }
    }
}
```

OUTPUT

Enter your age : 25

You are Welcome as a guest

[Also run the program for other values; g = 60 ; g = 9 ; g = 10]

Program 10 : A student would get a rank of different status depending upon the number of subjects in which the student scored distinction marks.

Distinction scored in number of subjects	Rank Status
5	Excellent
4	Outstanding
3	Brilliant
2	Bright
1	Vivid
0	Good

Input the number of subjects in which a student scored distinction marks and print his/her rank status accordingly. Print "Invalid Input" for any other input.

```java
import java.util.*;
class Program
{
    void main()
    {
        Scanner sc = new Scanner (System.in);  int n ;
        System.out.println("Enter the number of subjects in which the student has scored distinction marks: ");      n = sc.nextInt();
        switch (n)
        {
            case 5  : System.out.print("Excellent");
                    break;
            case 4  : System.out.print("Outstanding");
                    break;
            case 3  : System.out.print("Brilliant");
                    break;
            case 2  : System.out.print("Bright");
                    break;
            case 1  : System.out.print("Vivid");
                    break;
            case 0  : System.out.print("Good");
                    break;
            default : System.out.print("Invalid Input" );
        }
    }
}
```

OUTPUT : For student to execute and observe for various values of n.

Program 11 : A Shoe Company was promoting their sales on New Year 2020 offer.

For each customer, input the purchase amount and the date of birth (date in d, month in m, year in y).

If date is 15 then give a discount of 15% on purchase amount.

If date is 26 then give a discount of 26% on purchase amount.

For other customers, give a discount of 10% on purchase amount.

```java
import java.util.*;
class Program
{
    void main()
    {
```

```java
double p = 0, = dd, a = 0; Scanner sc = new Scanner (System.in);   int d, m, y;
System.out.print("\n Enter Purchase amount : ");    p = sc.nextDouble();
System.out.print("\n Enter date of birth (d, m, y): ");
d = sc.nextInt();   m = sc.nextInt();    y = sc.nextInt();
switch (d)
{
    case 15 : dd = 15.0/100 * p ;
            a = p - dd;
        System.out.println(" Congratulations! You get a discount of ₹ " + dd );
        System.out.println(" Your amount payable is ₹  " + a );
        break ;
    case 26 : dd = 26.0/100 * p ;
            a = p - dd;
        System.out.println(" Congratulations! You get a discount of ₹" + dd);
        System.out.println(" Your amount payable is ₹  " + a );
        break;
    default :  dd = 10.0/100 * p ;
            a = p - dd;
        System.out.println(" You get a discount of ₹ " + dd );
        System.out.println(" Your amount payable is ₹  " + a );
    }
  }
}
```

OUTPUT

Enter Purchase amount : 1000
Enter date of birth (d, m, y): 15
2
1995
Congratulations! You get a discount of ₹ 150.0
Your amount payable is ₹ 850.0

Note :

The above program can be optimized, as shown below :

```java
import java.util.*;
class Program
{
    void main()
    {
        double p = 0, dd = 0, a = 0; Scanner sc = new Scanner (System.in);
        int d, m, y;
        System.out.print("\n Enter Purchase amount : ");    p = sc.nextDouble();
```

```
        System.out.print("\n Enter date of birth (d, m, y): ");
        d = sc.nextInt();   m = sc.nextInt();    y = sc.nextInt();
        switch (d)
        {
            case 15 :  dd = 15.0/100 * p ;
                    break;
            case 26 : dd = 26.0/100 * p ;
                    break;
            default :  dd = 10.0/100 * p ;
        }

                a = p - dd;
        System.out.println(" Congratulations! You get a discount of ₹" + dd );
        System.out.println(" Your amount payable is ₹  " + a );

    }

}
```

Program 12 : A calculation based job has some choices as given below :

Choice ch = 1 : Input time in hours & minutes and convert it to total min [1hr = 60 min]

Choice ch = 2 : Input temperature in Celsius and convert it to Fahrenheit [C/5 = (F-32)/9]

Choice ch = 3 : Input length in Feet and convert it into cm. [1Feet = 30.48 cm]
Input the choice (ch), and accordingly take other inputs and perform calculation and output.

```
import java.util.*;
class Program
{
    void main( )
    {
        Scanner sc = new Scanner (System.in);  int ch ;
        System.out.print("\n Enter Choice : ");  ch = sc.nextInt();
        switch (ch)
        {
            case 1   :    int hr, min , tm;
                System.out.println(" Enter Hr, min : ");
                hr = sc.nextInt();
                min = sc.nextInt();
                tm = hr * 60 + min ;
                System.out.print (" Total min = " + tm);
                break;
            case 2   :    double C, F;
```

```java
            System.out.print(" Enter Celsius value : ");
            C = sc.nextDouble();
            F = ( C * 9.0/5.0 + 32 ) ;
            System.out.print(" Corresponding Fahrenheit temp : " + F);
            break;
        case 3 :    int Ft; double cm;
            System.out.print(" Enter how many feet : ");
            Ft = sc.nextInt();
            cm = Ft * 30.48 ;
            System.out.print(Ft + " Feet  = " + cm + " centimeter" );
            break;
        default :   System.out.print(" Wrong choice" );
      }
    }
}
```

OUTPUT

Enter Choice : 3

Enter how many feet : 10

10 Feet = 304.8 centimeter

Program 13 : A public bus service has ticket fare depending upon the distance. Input the fare by a passenger and print the distance travelled using the following chart :

Fare f (in₹)	Distance d (in km)
10	d <= 6
15	d > 6 and d <= 10
20	d> 10

```java
import java.util.*;
class Program
{
    void main()
    {
        Scanner sc = new Scanner (System.in);  int f ;
        System.out.println("Enter Ticket Fare : ");
        f = sc.nextInt();
        switch (f)
        {
            case 10 : System.out.print("Distance is <= 6 km.");
                    break;
            case 15 : System.out.print("Distance is > 6 km and <= 10 km.");
                    break;
```

```
            case 20 :  System.out.print("Distance is > 10 km");
                        break;
            default :  System.out.print("Invalid Fare Amount");
        }
    }
}
```

OUTPUT

Enter Ticket Fare:15

Distance is > 6 km and<= 10 km.

Exercise : Given the following code, complete the program

```
switch (mk)
{
    case 40 :   System.out.print("Just the Pass mark");
                break;
    case 60 :   System.out.print("First Division");
                break;
    case 80 :   System.out.print("Distinction");
                break;
    case 100 : System.out.print("Shining Star");
}
```

On Ternary Operator

Program 14 : In a group of people, a study revealed that the happiness factor (HF) depended on the amount of time spent (TS) together with a friend (F). It was evaluated in a formula:

```
HF = TS * 6        if F = 0
HF = TS * 12       otherwise
Input TS & F and print HF.
```

```java
import java.util.*;
class Program
{
    void main()
    {
        Scanner sc = new Scanner (System.in); int TS, F, HF;
        System.out.println("Enter Time Spent : ");  TS = sc.nextInt();
        System.out.println("Enter Friend value  : "); F = sc.nextInt();
        HF = ( F == 0) ? (TS * 6) : (TS * 12) ;
        System.out.print("Happiness Factor = " + HF );
    }
}
```

OUTPUT

Enter Time Spent: 12

Enter Friend value: 4

Happiness Factor = 144

Program 15 : Input three numbers and store the smallest of the three in S.

```java
import java.util.*;
class Program
{
    void main()
    {
        Scanner sc = new Scanner (System.in); double A, B, C, S ;
        System.out.println("Enter Number 1 : ");  A = sc.nextDouble();
        System.out.println("Enter Number 2 : ");  B = sc.nextDouble();
        System.out.println("Enter Number 3 : ");  C = sc.nextDouble();
        S = ( A< B) ? A : B ;
        S = ( C< S ) ? C : S ;
        System.out.println("Smallest is : " + S );
    }
}
```

OUTPUT

Enter Number 1 : 4.1

Enter Number 2 : 6.5

Enter Number 3 : 8.4

Smallest is   : 4.1

Program 16 : The value of K depended on P, Q such that

K = 10   , when P != Q   and   P is even

K = 20, when   P != Q   and   P is odd

K = 30   otherwise

```java
import java.util.*;
class Program
{
    void main()
    {
        Scanner sc = new Scanner (System.in); double P, Q, K ;
        System.out.println("Enter P : ");  P = sc.nextDouble();
        System.out.println("Enter Q : ");  Q = sc.nextDouble();
        K = ( P != Q )? ( (P%2 == 0) ? 10 : 20 ) : 30 ;
        System.out.println("K : " + K );
    }
}
```

OUTPUT

Enter P : 17

Enter Q : 12

K   : 20.0

Program 17 : Input the weight of two boxes in variables w1 and w2. Store the weight of the heavier box in variable hw. Print hw. Use ternary operator.

```java
//Use of Ternary Operator
import java.util.*;
class ProgG
{
    void main()
    {
        int w1 = 0, w2 = 0, hw = 0;
        Scanner sc = new Scanner (System.in) ;
        System.out.print("\n Enter the height of the 1st box : ");  w1 = sc.nextInt();
        System.out.print("\n Enter the height of the 2nd box : "); w2 = sc.nextInt();
        hw = (w1>w2) ? w1 : w2 ;
        System.out.print("\n Weight of the heavier box is " + hw);
    }
}
```

OUTPUT

Enter the height of the 1st box : 75

Enter the height of the 2nd box : 91

Weight of the heavier box is 91

Enter other sets of data and observe the output.

SUMMARY

- A conditional work is done only if the condition is true. In case a condition is false, either do nothing or do something else.
- There are 6 Relational Operators in Java : > < >= <= == !=
- There are 3 Logical Operators in Java : ! (Not)   && (And) || (Or)
- There are 3 conditional Statements in Java :
    - if....else statement
    - switch....case statement
    - ternary operator
- Conditional statement if....else, is used mainly in cases where a condition decides what will be the next course of action.
- Switch....case conditional statement is used in cases where the comparison is of equality only.

- In Switch....case statement, default becomes active when none of the cases match.
- In switch....case statement, fall through occurs if break statement is not given and then, all the statements that appear below the matching case, get executed.
- Ternary operator is used for small conditional cases.

SOLVED QUESTIONS

1. **What are relational operators?**

   Answer : Relational Operators help in creating a conditions.

   Java has six relational operators, shown in the following table :

Operator	Use	Operator	Use
>	Greater than	<=	Less than or equal to
<	Less than	==	Comparison of Equality
>=	Greater Than or Equal to	!=	Comparison of Inequality

2. **What are logical operators ?**

   Answer : Logical Operators help to connect more than one condition.

   Java has three logical operators, shown in the following table :

Operator	Use	Result
!	NOT	Reverses the result of a given condition
&&	AND	Result is True only if all the conditions are True
||	OR	Result is True if any one of the conditions is True

3. **What is a composite condition ?**

   Answer : A condition may be single or composite. A composite condition is made up of multiple conditions which are connected by using Logical Operators (AND and OR).

4. **Name the conditional statements of Java.**

   Answer : Java has three Conditional Statements –

   (a) if...else   (b) switch...case   (c) ternary operator

5. **In switch....case statement, what is the use of 'default' ?**

   Answer : Statement 'default' becomes active when none of the cases match. Default and the block present under it should appear at last.

   Default in switch...case is optional. Without its presence, there will be no action in the switch...case block, when none of the cases will match.

6. **What is fall through in switch case ?**

   Answer : If break is not given at the end of a case, then, all the statements that appear below the matching case, get executed. This situation is called Fall Through.

7. **What are the differences between if....else and switch....case statement ?**

Answer :

S.N.	if...else	switch...case
1.	All relational operators (greater than, less than, etc) can be used	Only comparison of equality operator is used
2.	Two variables can be compared	Only a variable and a constant can be compared
3.	Multiple conditions can be connected by using logical operators	Multiple conditions using logical operators cannot be connected
4.	All data types are allowed	Variables of type integer (byte, short, int, long) and char can only be used
5.	Preferred in cases where there are conditions other than equality comparison	Preferred in cases where there are simple conditions of equality
6.	Gives more variety and is better for bigger and complicated situations	Gives less variety and is better for smaller and simpler situations
7.	No use of break. Fall through not possible but brackets must match	Break is needed to avoid fall through

8. **Write down the conditions for the following situations :**

   (a) if the marks are equal to 40 then, print just the pass marks

```
if( m == 40)
{
    System.out.print (" Just the pass marks." );
}
```

   (b) if the marks are more than or equal to 40 then, print "pass" else print "fail"

```
if ( m >= 40)
{
    System.out.print (" Pass. " );
}
else
{
    System.out.print (" Fail. " );
}
```

   (c) if the age is more than 59 then print "Senior Citizen" else print "Citizens"

```
if ( a> 59 )
{
    System.out.print (" Senior Citizen" );
}
else
{
    System.out.print (" Citizen" );
}
```

EXERCISE

Question 1. Answer the following :

(a) Name the three types of loops.

(b) What are relational operators ? Which are they and what is their usage ?

(c) What are logical operators ? Which are they and what is their usage ?

(d) What is fall through ?

(e) What is the use of "default" in switch....case statement? What is its equivalent in "if..else" statement ? Show using an example.

(f) Write any four differences between if..else and switch...case statement.

Question 2. Given below are code statements that use ternary operator. What will be the value of R in each case :

(a) R = (25>30) ? 100 : 400;

(b) R = (102 == 102) ? 200 : 100;

(c) R = (75 < 100) ? 100 : 300 ;

(d) R = (2056 != 2056) ? 11 : 22 ;

Question 3. Given below are some program codes. Write their output :

```java
(a) int p = 55, q=45;
    if ( (p-5) > (q+5) )
    {
        System.out.print("Vaduz");
    }
    else
    {
        System.out.print("Liechtenstein");
    }
(b) int fb = 45 ;
    switch ( fb )
    {
        case 65 : System.out.print(" Finland ");
                break;
        case 45 : System.out.print(" France ");
                break;
        case 55 : System.out.print(" Fiji");
                break;
        default : System.out.print(" Flora ");
    }
```

```
(c)  int a = 100, b = 40 , c  = 5 ;
     if ( ( b + c )  <  a )
     {
         if( a % c == 0)
         {
             System.out.print("Vilnius");
         }
         else
         {
             System.out.print("Lithuania");
         }
     }
     else
     {
         System.out.print("Europe");
     }

(d)  long b = 65 , d = 8;
     if ( b > ( d * 8 ) )
     {
         b = b – (d * 5);
         if ( b >  d)
         {
             b = b – d;
         }
         else
         {
             b = b + d;
         }
     }
     System.out.print("San Marino" + b) ;
```

Question 4. Rewrite the following codes after debugging them and underline the changes made :

```
(a)  if ( p = 9 )                          (b)  if ( q <> 9 )
     {                                           {
         System.out.print ( " Nine );                System.out.print   ("   Not"
     }                                                               Nine ");
                                                 }
```

(c) if (w => 9)
```
     {
             System.out.print ( " Beyond
                               Nine" );
     }
```

(d) if (t ! 9)
```
     {
             System.out.print (' No' );
     }
```

(e) switch (k)
```
     {
         Case   23   :    System.out.
                          print("Red");
                          break ;
         Default   :      System.out.
                          print("Blue");
     }
```

(f) Switch (m)
```
     {
             case 9 : system.out.print(99);
                      break ;
             default : system.out.print(22);
     }
```

(g) if (w > 9)
```
     {
             System.out.print   (   "Above
                               Nine" );
     else
     System.out.print ( " Below Nine" );
     }
```

(h) d = (p > q) : p ? q ;

(i) g = (h != 0 ? 10) : 20;

(j) r = (p = 5) ? 8 : 4;

Question 5. Write a program for the following :

(a) Roshni purchased two books from a 'Book Fair'. She also availed discounts on the books. The books on which the printed price was more than 1000 the discount was 35% and for others, discount was 10%.

Input the printed price of the two books she purchased. Print the discount she got on each book. Print the total amount she paid.

(b) Surya purchased a guitar and a tabla upon selling his old SLR digital camera. Input the cost of the guitar and tabla and the selling price of his camera. Print whether he incurred profit or loss. Also print the profit or loss percent. Given that

profit percent = profit / (total cost price) * 100

loss percent   = loss / (total cost price) * 100

(c) In a Drama class, one special coach used to come on Monday and Thursday. The days of the week were numbered as 0 for Sunday, 1 for Monday, 2 for Tuesday, …, 6 for Saturday.

Input the day number and print the day name. Also print whether the special coach will come that day or not. Use Switch Case statement.

(d) Input two integer variables M and L. Verify whether variable M is a factor of variable L or not. If M is a factor of L, then print whether it is an even factor or an odd factor. If M is not a factor of L, then just print "Not a factor".

(e) A number (say **V**) is called a Stavensev number if it is (greater than 700 and a multiple of 77 at the same time) or (it is less than 77 and a factor of 700 at the same time).

Enter a number in variable **V** and verify whether **V** is a Stavensev number or not. [Example: 784, 10 and more]

(f) Temperature can be measured in two units, Celsius and Kelvin. Input the temperature in Celsius, convert it to Kelvin and print it. Given the formula

C = K + 273

(g) A new magazine was inviting advertisements at an introductory offer. A flat discount of 5% was offered on price of each advertisement. Moreover, if the advertisement was for a full page, an additional discount of 4% was given on the discounted price. Input the price of an advertisement in variable p and also whether it is a full page advertisement or not in variable fp (1 for yes). Print the discounted price.

(h) According to a study of human psychology, the approximate level of emotion in a person can be calculated using the age (say A) and height (say H) of the person, using the following formula:

E = 5 +(0.45 * A + 0.5 H) / (A+H), if A<= 12

E = 15 + (0.26 * A + 0.35 * H) / (2*A – H) otherwise

Input the values of A , H. Calculate the value of E using the criteria given above.

ITERATIVE CONSTRUCTS IN JAVA

Contents

INTRODUCTION

When a work is done over and over again, it is said to be in a loop. There are many instances of loops going around us. For example, when small children learn nursery rhymes, the songs are played in a loop. There is another example that happens at the security check of the passengers going to board a flight. The security personnel perform checking on all the customers one by one in a loop.

15×1	=	15
15×2	=	30
15×3	=	45
15×4	=	60
15×5	=	75
15×6	=	90
15×7	=	105
15×8	=	120
15×9	=	135
15×10	=	150

There are many mathematical tasks where loops are used for better performance. For example, printing the multiplication table of a number, N, from 1 to 10. The process is simple, multiply N with each number ranging from 1 to 10 one by one and print the result each time.

Thus, we can say that loops are used to perform repetitive tasks. Let us now look into the detail of how loops are implemented.

WHAT IS A LOOP ?

A loop in Java, is a method that is used to execute a block of code repeatedly. A loop is a concept in which a code is executed repeatedly as long as a condition is valid.

Every loop has the following components :

Loop counter : A variable that counts the number of times a loop is repeating.

Initialization : The initial value of a loop counter.

Test Condition : The criteria that indicates whether the loop should repeat or not.

Updation : The modification of the loop counter.

There are three types of loops in Java : (i) for (ii) while (iii) do.. while

These loops lie under two categories :

(i) Entry Controlled Loop

This kind of loop verifies the loop condition before entering the loop. If the condition is initially false, then the loop does not get executed at all. **for** and **while** loops are entry controlled loops.

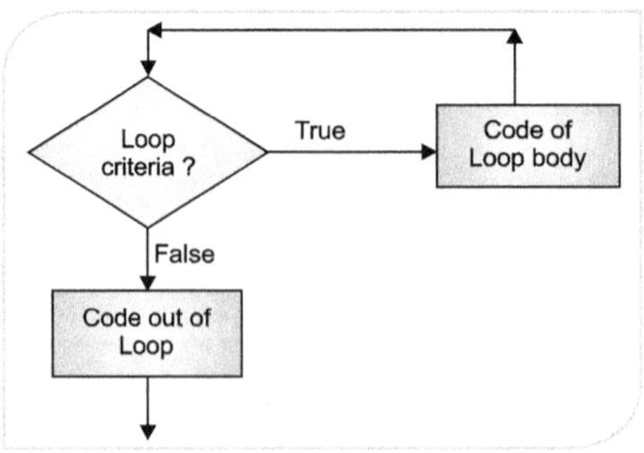

Fig. 6.1

(ii) Exit Controlled Loop

This kind of loop first allows the control to enter the loop and then verifies the loop condition. If the condition is initially false, the loop gets executed at least once. **do..while** loop is an exit controlled loop.

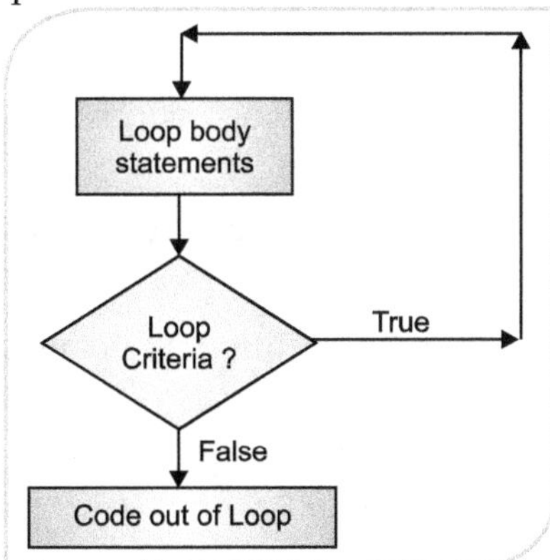

Fig. 6.2

We will learn how to implement the loops one by one.

for Loop

This loop is used when the number of times the task has to be repeated is known. It is an iteration statement in which there is an option of declaring and initializing the loop counter, verification of its validity in condition and incrementing/decrementing the loop counter. Every for loop has a loop counter which counts the number of iterations of the loop.

It executes the block of code only when the condition is true. It is an **entry controlled** loop.

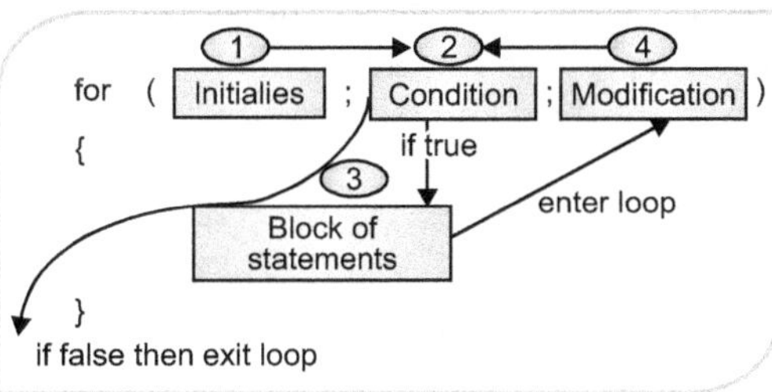

Fig. 6.3

Syntax :

```
for( initialization ; condition ; increment)
{
    Block of statements
}
```

Example:	OUTPUT
`for( k = 1;  k<= 10;  k = k+1)`	
`{`	Hello Roll Number 1
`    System.out.println(" Hello Roll Number  " + k);`	Hello Roll Number 2
`}`	...
	Hello Roll Number 10

Here initialization k=1; condition k<=10; means until k is greater than 10, it executes the statements under the loop; increment k=k+1; it increments the value of k by 1.

Loop Counter

It is a variable that counts the number of iterations. Every for loop has a loop counter (**k** in the above example).

In general, variables i, j, k are used as loop counters.

Note :

- The block of initialization and increment can contain more than one statement using comma operator.

    for(initialization1, initialization 2; condition ;increment 1, increment2)
    {

    Block of statements

    }

    [Explained in later programs]

For Loop Variations

There are mainly four variations of for loop -

I.   Multiple Initialization and Update Expression
II. Optional Expression
III. Infinite Loop
IV. Delay or Empty Loop

Let us now look at them in detail –

I. Multiple Initialization and Update Expression : A for-loop permits multiple variables to be initialized and incremented/decremented. Hence, the block of initialization and increment can contain more than one statement using comma operator. Note that, it allows data of same data-type only.

Syntax :

for (initialization1, initialization2 ;   condition ;   increment 1, increment2)
{

    Block-of-statements

}

Example :

for (int p = 1, q = 10 ;   p < 5 ; p= p+1 , q = q+2)
{

        System.out.println(" P = " + p + " and Q = " + q);

}

OUTPUT :

                    P = 1 and Q = 10
                    P = 2 and Q = 12
                    P = 3 and Q = 14
                    P = 4 and Q = 16

Example : The following code will show an error because of the various data-types in declaration. Observe the error and the correction

```
for ( double b = 100.0 , int q = 10 ;  b >= 10 ;  b = b - 10 , q = q+2  )
{
    System.out.println ("B = "+ b +"  and  Q = " + q);
}
```

Error : Variables b, q should have been of the same data-type, either both int or both double.

II. Optional Expression : Although a for loop has 3 slots for placing initialization, condition and increment/decrement, It gives an option to keep them empty if needed.

Example

```
int k = 10 ;
for ( ;   k>= 5  ; k - - )
{
    System.out.println( " value  of k   = " + k ) ;
}
```

Note :

- The slots must be reserved otherwise it will give errors.

Example : Observe that there are only two slots, separated by one ; and so it will give syntax error.

```
int w = 20 ;
for (w <= 30   ; w++ )
{
    System.out.println( "W = " + w ) ;
}
```

Note :

- The content of any empty slot must be present in some other relevant place.

III. Infinite Loop : A loop is called an Infinite Loop if it repeats its statement block endlessly that is if the condition in the loop never evaluates to false. It is generally considered a logical error but sometimes it can be utilized for doing tasks that are always ON, such as an ATM service, ticket counter service etc.

Example

```
for ( ;  ; )                                for ( int p =15; p>1  ; p++ )
{                                           {
    System.out.println ( "Hello" ) ;            System.out.println ( p ) ;
}                                           }
```

IV. Delay or Empty Loop : A loop is called an Empty Loop if it contains no code in it. It can be considered as a logical error except for situations where it is written intentionally, when it is called a Delay loop.

A Delay loop is an Empty Loop that does no task but iterates a certain number of times, giving a wait effect in a program. One application is to show an output screen for some time.

Example

```
for ( int w=1; w<50000000 ; w++ ) ;      for ( int p =1; p<100000  ; p++ )
                                          {

                                          }
```


Program 1 : Program to print the odd numbers from 501 to 515.

```java
// Odd numbers from 501 to 515
import java.io.*;
class ProgA
{
    void main()
    {
        System.out.print("  The ODD numbers from 501 to 515 are -- \n" );
        for(int k = 501;   k<=515;   k = k+2)
        {
            System.out.print(" " + k );
        }
    }
}
```

OUTPUT

The ODD numbers from 501 to 521 are --

501 503 505 507 509 511 513 515

Review of Increment/Decrement & Shorthand Operators (detail in chapter 7)

In Java, we can write p = p + 1 also as p++. Similarly, we can write p = p – 1 also as p-- .

++ is the increment operator and -- is the decrement operator. They are used only for increasing/decreasing value of a variable by 1.

Shorthand operators can change the value of a variable by various values.

a += 5   is same as   a = a + 5

Program 2 : Program code to print the numbers.

710   700   690   680   670   660   650   640   630   620   610   600

```java
for( k = 710;   k >= 600;   k -= 10)
{
    System.out.print ("      " + k );
}
```

Practice Program : Write a program code to print the numbers.

11   22   33   44   55

Program 3 : Program showing the use of comma operator in a for loop.

```java
import java.io.*;
class ProgCA
{
    void main ()
    {
        System.out.print(" " );
        for(int w = 9, m = 5 ; w >= 1 ;  w=w-2, m=m+1)
        {
            System.out.println("W = " + w + "   M = " + m );
        }
    }
}
```

OUTPUT

Output of Comma in a for loop

W = 9   M = 5
W = 7   M = 6
W = 5   M = 7
W = 3   M = 8
W = 1   M = 9

Here, we can see that initialization and increment have the two statements that are written using comma operator.

Program 4 : Program to print the following series up to n terms, where n is entered by the user.

20   40   60 80 ...

Program Idea :

(i)   This program introduces term numbers and term values.

(ii) The term numbers are counted from 1 to n. Total number of terms (n) is a variable and is a user input. Say, if n = 7 then the series goes up to 7 terms.

Term Value	20	40	60	80	100	120	...
Term Number	1	2	3	4	5	6	upto n terms

(iii) For each term, term value = term number * 20

```java
//Print the series   20    40    60    80 ...up to n terms
import java.util.*;
class ProgD
{
    void main()
    {
        int n=0, tn = 0, tv = 0;
        Scanner sc = new Scanner (System.in);
```

```
        System.out.print("\n Enter the total number of terms (n) : ");
        n = sc.nextInt();
        for(tn = 1;   tn<= n;   tn++)
        {
            tv = tn * 20;
            System.out.print(" .. " + tv );
        }
    }
}
```

OUTPUT

Enter the total number of terms (n) : 10
.. 20 ..40 ..60 ..80 ..100 ..120 ..140 ..160 ..180 .. 200

Program 5 : Above program with another logic

// Each value is 20 more than the previous value. So, new term value = previous term value + 20

```
tv = 0 ; ............
for(tn = 1;   tn<= n;   tn++)
{
    tv = tv + 20;
    System.out.print(" .. " + tv );
}
```

Program 6 : Program to print the following series up to n terms, where n is entered by the user.   6   12   24   48   96   ...

Program Idea :

(i)   The series is beginning with 6. Each next term is the double of the previous term.

(ii) The term values are easily related to their previous value, rather than the term number.

(iii) For each term, new term value = previous term value * 2

Term Value	6	12	24	48	96	...
Term Num	1	2	3	4	5	upto n term

(similar to the previous program)

```
tv = 6;
............
for(tn = 1;   tn<= n;   tn++)
{
    System.out.print(" .. " + tv );
    tv = tv * 2;
}
```

OUTPUT : Verify the output by entering n as 5

Program 7 : Program to print the sum of 1st n natural numbers, where n is entered by the user. This series is also called **Summation Series.** $\quad 1 + 2 + 3 + 4 + ... + n$

Program Idea :

(i)   In this series the term numbers coincide with the term values.

(ii) The sum of the series is calculated by using another variable, (tsum), which starts with 0 and **adds the next term** to it each time.

(iii) For each term, new sum = previous sum + next term

Term Val	1	2	3	4	5	...
Term Num	1	2	3	4	5	upto n terms

TSum   0+1=1   1+2=3   3+3=6   6+4=10   10+5=15

(iv) The program has only one output, the sum of the series, to be printed. The output statement, therefore, should occur out of the loop bounds.

```java
//Print the sum of the series     1 + 2 + 3 + 4 + ... + n
import java.util.*;
public class ProgG
{
    void main()
    {
        int n=0, tn = 0, tsum = 0; Scanner sc = new Scanner (System.in);
        System.out.print("\n Enter total terms (n) : "); n = sc.nextInt();
        for(tn = 1;    tn<= n;    tn++)
        {
            tsum = tsum + tn;
        }
        System.out.print(" The sum of the series = " + tsum );
    }
}
```

OUTPUT

Enter the total number of terms (n) : 9

The sum of the series = 45

Enter the total number of terms (n) : 5

The sum of the series = 15

Program 8 : Program to print the product of 1st n natural numbers, where n is entered by the user. This series is also called **Factorial Series.** $1 * 2 * 3 * 4 * ... * n$

Program Idea :

(i)   In this series the term numbers coincide with the term values.

(ii) The product of the series is calculated by using another variable, tpro, which starts with 1 and **multiplies the next term** to it each time.

(iii) For each term, new product = previous product * next term.

Term Value	1	2	3	4	5	...
Term Number	1	2	3	4	5	upto n terms

TPro   1*1=1   1*2=2   2*3=6   6*4=24   24*5=120

(iv) The program has only one output, the product of the series, to be printed. The output statement, therefore, should occur out of the loop bounds.

(v) Datatype long is preferred for storing huge result.

(similar to the previous program)

```
..... tpro = 1;
for(tn = 1;   tn<= n;   tn++)
{
    tpro = tpro *tn;
}
    System.out.print(" The product of the series = " + tpro );
```

OUTPUT ; verify the output with n = 6

Program 9 : Program to print the following series. This series is also called the Fibonacci series.

1   1   2   3   5   8   13   21   ...

Program Idea :

(i)   The term numbers not same as term values.

(ii) From the 3rd to the last term, each term is the sum of its previous two terms (loop 3 to n).

(iii) The working of the loop is as shown -

Note :

1	1	2	3	5	8	13	21	.... upto n
term1	term2	term3						
	term1							
		term2						
		term3						

Each time, first (term1 gets term2) then (term2 gets term3) and then (term3 = term1 + term2).

```
//Print the Fibonacci series   1   1   2   3   5   8   13   21   ...
import java.util.*;
public class ProgI
{
    void main()
    {
        int n, tn, term1 = 1, term2 = 1, term3 =0;Scanner sc = new Scanner (System.in);
        System.out.print("\n Enter the total number of terms (n) : ");
        n = sc.nextInt();
        System.out.print(" The Fibonacci series upto term " + n + " is  \n ");
        System.out.print( term1 + "    " + term2 + "  ");
        for(tn = 3;   tn<= n;   tn++)
```

```java
        {
            term3 = term1 + term2;
            System.out.print( term3 + "   ");
            term1 = term2;
            term2 = term3;
        }
    }
}
```

OUTPUT

Enter the total number of terms (n) : 6

The Fibonacci series upto term 6 is

1   1   2   3   5   8

Question. What will be the output of the above code if term1 = 5, term2 = 10 and n = 6 ?

Program 10 : Input marks obtained by 10 students. Calculate and print the average marks.

Program Idea :

(i) In this case, 10 marks have to be entered (case of input inside a loop).

(ii) The sum can be calculated by adding each mark to the total marks.

(iii) After entering all the marks, the loop terminates.

(iv) The average is to be calculated once outside the loop.

```java
import java.util.*;
public class LoopProgP
{
    void main()
    {
        int m=0, total = 0; double avg = 0.0;
        Scanner sc = new Scanner (System.in);
        for(int r = 1; r <= 10 ; r++)
        {
            System.out.print ("\n Enter marks of roll number " + r + " : ");
            m = sc.nextInt ();
            total = total + m ;
        }
            avg = total/10.0 ;
            System.out.print( "\n  Average :  " + avg ) ;
    }
}
```

OUTPUT

Enter marks of roll number 1 : 60

Enter marks of roll number 2 : 50

Enter marks of roll number 3 : 70

......   [... 40 50 60 80 40 80 90]

Average : 62.0

Program 11 : Print the cube of all the numbers from 21 to 31.

Program Idea :

(i) In this case, there will be multiple outputs (case of calculation & output inside a loop).

(ii) The range of numbers need to be generated using a for loop.

(iii) The cube has to be calculated for each iteration.

(iv) The output too has to be printed for each iteration.

```java
import java.util.*;
public class Program
{
    void main()
    {
        double r1, r2, c ;
        for(int k = 21; k <= 31; k++)
        {
            c = k*k*k ;
            System.out.println( k + " ^ 3 = " + c );
        }
    }
}
```

OUTPUT

21 ^ 3 = 9261.0	27 ^ 3 = 19683.0
23 ^ 3 = 12167.0	28 ^ 3 = 21952.0
24 ^ 3 = 13824.0	29 ^ 3 = 24389.0
25 ^ 3 = 15625.0	30 ^ 3 = 27000.0
26 ^ 3 = 17576.0	31 ^ 3 = 29791.0

While Loop

This loop is used when a task is to be repeated as long as a condition is valid. It evaluates the given condition first then executes the loop, till the condition holds true. It is an entry controlled loop. Here, the number of times the task has to be repeateds is not specifically known.

[Different loops have different application area though one loop can be converted to another.]

Syntax :

while (Condition)

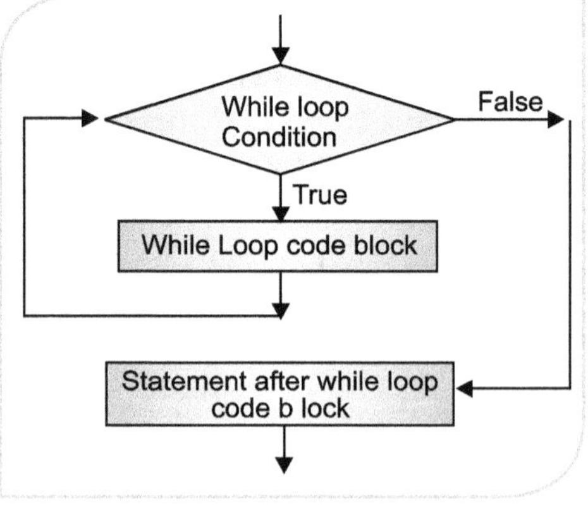

Fig. 6.4

```
{
    Block of statements
}
```

Observe the following example of a program code :

```
int value = 400;        //initialization
while ( value <= 500)  //condition
{
System.out.print( "      " + value);
value = value + 15;     //value modification
}
```

OUTPUT

400   415   430   445   460   475   490

Thus, we see that a while loop just tests a condition. The initialization is done before the loop begins. The value modification for the condition is done inside the loop.

Note :

- It is very imporant to take care of the value modification in a while loop, otherwise the loop becomes an infinite loop.

While Loop Variations

I. Infinite Loop

If we don't write the update expression in the loop then while loop executes the code infinite number of times.

```
while ( true )
{
    System.out.println ( "Hello" ) ;
}
```

```
int k = 10;
while ( k > 5 )
{
        System.out.println ( "Hello" ) ;
}
```

II. Empty Loop

```
while ( true ) ;
// Here, the loop body is empty,
// but it is an infinite loop
```

```
int k = 10;
while (  k <=15000 )
{
        k++ ;
}
```

Programs on while Loop

Program 12 : Program to print the digits of a number with a line gap.

Program Idea :

(i)   When a number (n) is divided by 10, the remainder is the last digit and the quotient is the first part without the last digit.

For example, n = 3496, divide by 10, remainder = 6, quotient = 349.

(ii) To print the digits of a number, a number is divided by 10, remainder gives the last digit, quotient gives the reduced number. The division is repeated till the number does not become 0.

Example :   n = 5842;

5842 >= 0	true	r = 2	print r	n = 584
584 >= 0	true	r = 4	print r	n = 58
58 >– 0	true	r = 8	print r	n = 5
5 >= 0	true	r = 5	print r	n = 0
0 > 0	false			

[use of integer division]

Note :

- Avoid changing the source number. [The program is shown below.]

```java
//Print the digits of a number
import java.util.*;
public class LoopProgJ
{
    void main()
    {
        int n=0, cn = 0, d = 0;
        Scanner sc = new Scanner (System.in);
        System.out.print("\nEnter the number : ");
        n = sc.nextInt();
        cn = n;
        System.out.print("The digits are ...\n" );
        while(cn>0)
        {
            d = cn % 10;
            System.out.print(d + "\n");
            cn = cn/10;
        }
    }
}
```

OUTPUT

```
Enter the number : 6482          Enter the number : 0
The digits are ...               The digits are ...
2
8
4
6
```

Note :

* The program prints no output if cm=0. But if the loop condition is changed to (cn< = 0), the loop turns to be an infinite loop. A do...while loop provides a solution to the above problem. That is shown in the next section.

Program 13 : Program to create the reverse of a number.

Program Idea :

(i)   To create a number, we can use the place value of its digits.

   Such as 7259 = 7 x 1000 + 2 x 100 + 5 x 10 + 9

(ii) To create a the reverse of a number, we can use the digits from the end one by one as shown

   n – the number; cn - copy of the number n, which changes each time

   r – the last digit each timerev – the new number each time (prev value x 10 + r)

   n = 5842

   cn = n;

5842 >= 0	true	r = 2	rev = 0 * 10 + r = 2	cn = 584
584 >= 0	true	r = 4	rev = 2 * 10 + r = 24	cn = 58
58 >= 0	true	r = 8	rev = 24 * 10 + r = 248	cn = 5
5 >= 0	true	r = 5	rev = 248 * 10 + r = 2485	cn = 0
0 > 0	false			

```java
//Create and print the reverse of a number
import java.util.*;
public class LoopProgK
{
    void main()
    {
        int n=0, cn = 0, r=0, rev = 0;
        Scanner sc = new Scanner (System.in);
        System.out.print("\nEnter the number : ");
        n = sc.nextInt();    cn = n;
        while(cn>0)
        {
            r = cn % 10;
            rev = rev * 10 + r;
            cn = cn/10;
        }
        System.out.print("\nThe reverse number of " + n + " is  " + rev);
    }
}
```

OUTPUT

Enter the number : 4926	Enter the number : 10048
The reverse number of 4926 is 6294	The reverse number of 10048 is 84001

Program 14. A number is called Palindrome if it is the same as its reverse. Input a number and verify whether it is a palindrome or not.

Program Idea :

(i)   The previous program shows how to create the reverse of a number.

(ii) To verify a Palindrome, a number's reverse should be compared to the number itself.

(iii) In the above logic, add a condition if (num == rev)for Palindrome.

(iv) Given ahead is the program code.

```java
//Verification of Palindrome ...
System.out.print("\nThe reverse number of " + n + " is  " + rev);
if ( n == rev)
{
    System.out.print ("\n The number " + n + " is Palindrome. " );
}
else
{
    System.out.print ("\n The number " + n + " is NOT Palindrome. " );
}
...
```

OUTPUT

Enter the number : 4926

The number of 4926 is NOT Palindrome.

Enter the number : 8008

The number of 8008 is Palindrome.

do ... while Loop

This loop is similar to a while loop with the difference that it gets executed at least once. This loop is applied in such cases where it is taken for granted that a task will take place at least once and will repeat as long as a condition is true. It is an exit controlled loop.

Syntax :

```java
do
{
    Block of statements
} while (condition);
```

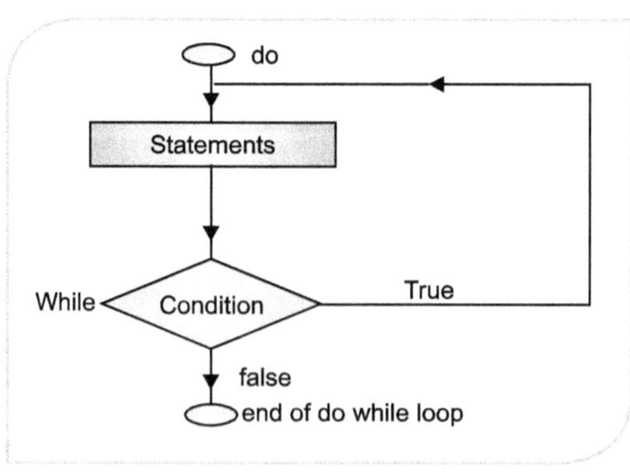

Fig. 6.5

120

Note :

- *Unlike the other two loop structures (for and while), do...while loop ends with a semicolon.*

Observe the following example of a program code :

```java
int val = 0;   //initialization
do
{
    System.out.print( " Enter an even number :   ");
    val = sc.nextInt() ;     //value modification
} while ( val%2 != 0);          //condition
```

Explanation of the above code :

(i)   Shown above, is an error trapping code.

(ii) A variable named **val** has to be filled up with an even number. The input of variable **val** takes place first time as a simple statement.

(iii) Then the condition is tested. If variable val turns out to be an odd number, then the loop repeats and the input is asked for again. The loop will repeat as long as the value entered in variable val is not even.

(iv) Thus, in this do...while loop, the task of input takes place first and then the validation take place. If invalid, the process is repeated.

do-while Loop Variations

I. Infinite Loop

If we don't write the update expression in the loop, then do - while loop executes the code infinite number of times.

```java
do
{
    System.out.println ( "Hello" );
} while (  true );
```

```java
int k = 10;
do
{
        System.out.println ( "Hello" );
} while (  k > 5 )
```

II. Empty Loop

```java
do
{

} while (  true );
```

```java
int k = 10;
do
{
        k++ ;
} while (  k <=1500 );
```

Program on do....while

Program 15 : Program to print the digits of a number with a space gap. Use do...while loop.

Program Idea :

(i)   The same program logic is applied this time as well, except that this time instead of while loop, do...while loop is used.

(ii) It is taken for granted that the number that is entered is valid.

(iii) When the program was done by using while loop, for n = 0, the loop condition was becoming false and there was no output.

(iv) With do...while loop, for n = 0, the loop will run first and then the condition will be tested. So the output will appear at least once.

```java
//Print the digits of a number
import java.util.*;
public class LoopProgM
{
    void main( )
    {
        int n=0, cn = 0, d = 0;
        Scanner sc = new Scanner (System.in);
        System.out.print("\n Enter the number : ");
        n = sc.nextInt(); cn = n;
        System.out.println("The digits are ..." );
        do
        {
            d = cn % 10;
            System.out.print(d + " ");
            cn = cn/10;
        } while(cn>0);
    }
}
```

OUTPUT

```
Enter the number : 6482      Enter the number : 0
The digits are ...           The digits are ...
2 8 4 6                      0
```

COMPARISON OF THE VARIOUS LOOP STATEMENTS

S.No.	for	While	Do-while
1.	It is an entry controlled loop.	It is an entry controlled loop.	It is an exit controlled loop.

2.	It first checks the condition and executes the block of code only when the condition is true.	It first checks the condition and then executes the block of code if the condition is true.	It exeutes block of code at least once.

3.	Syntax: for (initialization; condition; increment)
	{
	   Block of
	   statements
	}
		Syntax : while (condition)
		{
		   Block of
		   statement
		}
			Syntax : do
			{
			   Block of
			   statements
			} while (condition);

Question : When to use which loop ?

Answer : For loop   : When a task has to be repeated known number of times.

While loop   : When a task has to be repeated as long as a condition is valid.

Do-while loop : When a task has to b e done at least once and then repeated as long as a condition is valid.

INTER CONVERSION OF LOOPS

To convert from one loop to another, identify the initialization, condition and the updating of the loop counter.

Syntax of for Loop:

```
for(<initialisation>; <Condition>; <Increment/decrement>)
{
    <Loop Body>
}
```

Syntax of while loop:

```
<initialisation>
while (<Condition>)
{
    <Loop Body>
    <Increment/decrement>
}
```

Syntax of do..while:

```
<initialisation>
do
{
    <Loop Body><Increment/decrement>
} while (<condition>);
```

Note :

- Place respective value from for loop to while loop and vice versa to get the desired loop.

- Place respective value from for loop to do....while loop and vice versa to get the desired loop.
- In the similar manner place respective value from while loop to do....while loop and vice versa to get the desired loop.

Some Examples are

(1) Convert the for Loop into while and do..while Loop

The given code using for loop is

```
for ( k = 1; k<=10; k++ )
{
    System.out.print ( k +  "  ");
}
```

The code using while loop:

```
int k = 1;
while ( k<= 10 )
{
    System.out.print ( k +  "  "); k++ ;
}
```

The code using do..while loop:

```
int k = 1;
do
{
    System.out.print ( k +  "  "); k++ ;
} while ( k<= 10 ) ;
```

(2) Convert the do-while Loop into for Loop

The given code using do..while loop is

```
int i = 1;
int d = 5;
do
{
    d = d* 2;
    System.out.println (d);
    i++;
} while (i < = 5);
```

The code using for loop:

```
 int i, d=5;
for( i=1; i<=5; i++ )
{
    d = d*2 ;
    System.out.println(d) ;
}
```

124

(3) Convert the while Loop into the for Loop

The given code using while loop:

```java
int m = 5, n = 10;
while (n>=1)
{
    System.out.println(m*n);
    n-- ;
}
```

The code using for loop:

```java
int m=5, n;
for(n=10 ; n>=1 ; n--)
{
    System.out.println( m*n );
}
```

(4) Convert while Loop into do..while Loop

The given code using while loop:

```java
int h = 100;
while ( h > 0 )
{
    System.out.print( h + "   " ) ;
    h = h – 10 ;
}
```

The code using do..while loop:

```java
int h = 100;
do
{
    System.out.print( h + "   " ) ;
    h = h – 10 ;
} while ( h > 0 );
```

(5) Convert do..while Loop into while Loop

The given code using while loop:

```java
int j = 2048 ;
do
{
    System.out.print( j + "   " ) ;
    j = j / 2 ;
}while ( j > 0 ) ;
```

The code using while loop:

```java
int j = 2048 ;
while ( j > 0 )
{
```

```
        System.out.print( j + "   " ) ;
        j = j / 2 ;
    }
```

JUMP STATEMENTS

These statements are used to take the control to another location in the code. Java supports three jump statements break, continue and return[1]. Here, we will discuss break and continue statements.

The Break Statement in a Loop

The break statement causes a loop to terminate its iterations. Whenever a break is encountered, the control comes out to the statement next to the block of the loop.

Note :

- If break is used without any condition, the loop loses its effect.
- There is no effect of break in a condition block, since a condition does not repeat.

Syntax :

(i) break in a for loop :
```
for( initialization ; condition ; increment)
{
    Block1 ;
    if(condition)
    {
        break;
    }
    Block2;
}
    Block3;
```

(ii) break in a while loop
```
while ( condition )
{
    Block1 ;
    if(condition)
    {
        break;
    }
    Block2;
}
    Block3;
```

(iii) break in a do..while loop
```
do
{
    Block1;
    if(condition)
    {
        break;
    }
    Block2;
} while ( condition ) ;
Block3;
```

Program 16 A : Program to show the application of break statement in a for loop. [This is a demonstrating program. Run the program and see the output.]

```
// application of break in a for loop
```

---

1. Return statement will be discussed in X class.

```java
import java.util.*;
public class ProgNA
{
    void main()
    {   int j = 0;
        for( j = 100;   j <= 125;   j++)
        {
            if (j ==111)
            {
                break;
            }
                System.out.print("\n  Value of j = " + j );
        }
                System.out.print("\n  OUT OF THE LOOP Value of j = " + j );
    }
}
```

OUTPUT

- Had the conditional break not been there, the loop would have printed 100 to 125.

Program 16 B : Program to show the application of break statement in a while loop. [This is a demonstrating program. Run the program and see the output.]

```java
// application of break in a for loop
import java.util.*;
public class ProgNB
{
    void main()
    {   int j = 0;
        while ( j < 100 )
        {
            System.out.print(" "+ j );
            j++;
            if (j >= 60)
            break;
        }
            System.out.print("\n  OUT OF THE LOOP Value of j = " + j );
    }
}
```

The Continue Statement in a Loop

The continue statement causes the loop to skip the rest of the statements for that round and go to the next round of iteration.

(i) continue in a for loop :
```
for( initialization ; condition ; increment)
{
    Block1
    if(condition)
    {
        continue;
    }
        Block2;
}
    Block3;
```

(ii) continue in a while loop :
```
while ( condition )
{
    Block1
    if(condition)
    {
    continue;
    }
        Block2;
}
    Block3;
```

(iii) continue in a do...while loop :
```
do
{
    Block1;
    if(condition)
    {
        Continue;
    }
        Block2;
} while ( condition ) ;
    Block3;
```

Program 17: Program to show the application of 'continue' statement in a loop. [This is a demonstrating program.]

```
// application of continue in a for loop
import java.util.*;
public class ProgO
{
    void main()
    {
        int j = 0;
        for( j = 100;  j <= 125;  j++)
        {
            if (j ==121)
            {
                continue;
            }
```

```
        System.out.print("\n  Value of j = " + j );
    }
        System.out.print("\n  OUT OF THE LOOP Value of j = " + j );
    }
}
```

OUTPUT

- The entire range from 100 to 125 except 121 is printed.

INFINITE LOOP

A loop that repeats infinite times is called an infinite loop. It is a general error situation where a loop goes on and on for the infinite number of times. Any of the three loops may become infinite.

Example 1 :
```
for( j = 100;   j <= 125;   j - -)
{
        System.out.print ("  " + j );
}
```

Example 2 :
```
k = 200;
while(  k>100)
{
        System.out.print(" " + k );
        k++;
}
```

Example 3 :
```
k = 200;
do
{
    System.out.print(" " + k );
    k++;
} while( k>100);
```

Example 4 :
```
for( j = 12;   j >= 10;   j ++)
{
        System.out.print ("  " + j );
}
```

Example 5 :
```
k = 1;
wihle( k<=20)
{
    System.out.print("\n  Value of k = "
                        + k );
}
```

Note :

- Shown in example 5, is a common error found in use of while loop, where the value of the counter has not been changed.
- In higher programming, infinite loop has specific application area.

A DUMMY LOOP OR AN EMPTY LOOP

It is a loop that does not have any task in it. But an empty loop is not an infinite loop. One application area of empty loop is in "to wait or to delay ".

Example : for(j = 1;   j <= 1000;   j++) ;

Note :

- The terminator at the end shows that the loop has no task.

Exercise : Justify which is finite loop and which is infinite loop.

```
for(i = 1; i<=10; i++)
{
    if (i == 5 )
    continue;
    System.out.print(" I = " + i);
}
```

```
while ( i<=10)
{
    System.out.print(" before I = " + i);
    if (i == 5 )
    continue;
    System.out.print(" after I = " + i);
    i++;
}
```

PROGRAMS FOR PRACTICE

What will be the output of the following programs ? Also modify the programs by taking input of n.

Program 18 :

```
public class LoopProgP
{
    void main()
    {
        int n= 2354 , cn = 0, r = 0, re = 0;cn = n;
        while ( cn> 0 )
        {
            r = cn % 10;
            re = re * 100 + r;
            cn = cn/10;
        }
        System.out.print( "\n Result :" + re );
    }
}
```

Program 19 :

```
public class LoopProgQ
{
```

```java
    void main()
    {
        int n = 2354 ,  cn = 0, r = 0, rev = 0;   cn = n;
        while ( cn> 0 )
        {
            r = cn % 10 ;
            rev = rev * 10 + r ;
            cn = cn/100 ;
            System.out.print( "\n R " + r + " rev " + rev);
        }
            System.out.print( "\n  Result :  " + rev ) ;
    }
}
```

Program 20 :

```java
public class LoopProgR
{
    void main()
    {
        int n = 2354 ,  cn = 0, r = 0, rev = 0;   cn = n;
        while ( cn> 0 )
        {
            r = cn % 100 ;
            rev = rev * 10 + r ;
            cn = cn/10 ;
            System.out.print( "\n R " + r + " rev " + rev);
        }
            System.out.print( "\n  Result :  " + rev ) ;
    }
}
```

Program 21 :

```java
public class LoopProgS
{
    void main()
    {
        int p = 10;
        for ( int k = 9; k >= 1 ; k = k-2 )
        {
            System.out.print( "\n K : " + k + " P : " + p );
            p = p+5 ;
        }
    }
}
```

Program 22 :

```java
public class LoopProgT
{
    void main()
    {
        int a = 2, b = 9, sum = 0;
        for ( int k = 1 ; k <= 5 ; k++ )
        {
            sum = a + b ;
            System.out.print( sum + " "  );
            a++ ;
            b = sum ;
        }
    }
}
```

Program 23 :

```java
public class LoopProgT
{
    void main()
    {
        int a = 5463, p = 1 , d = 0;
        for ( int k = 1 ; k <= 4 ; k++ )
        {
            d = a % 10 ;
            System.out.print( d + " "  );
            p = p * d ;
            a /= 10 ;
        }
            System.out.print( "\nP = " + p );
    }
}
```

Program 24 :

```java
public class LoopProgU
{
    void main()
    {
        int n = 1234 ,  cn = 0, r = 0, rev = 0;   cn = n;
        do
        {
            r = cn % 10 ;
            rev = rev * 10 + r ;
            cn = cn/10 ;
        } while ( cn< 0 ) ;
            System.out.print( "\n  Result :  " + rev );
    }
}
```

SUMMARY

- Loops are used to perform repetitive tasks.
- **Loop counter** : A variable that counts the number of times a loop is repeating.
- **Initialization** : The initial value of a loop counter.
- **Test Condition** : The criteria that indicates whether the loop should repeat or not.
- **Updation**: The modification of the loop counter.
- There are three types of loops in Java (i) for (ii) while (iii) do....while
- Entry Controlled Loop is a kind of loop which verifies the loop condition before entering the loop. If the condition is initially false, then the loop does not get executed at all. In Java, for and while are entry controlled loops.
- Exit Controlled Loop is a kind of loop that first allows the control to enter and then verifies the loop condition. If the condition is initially false, the loop gets executed at least once. In Java, do...while is an exit controlled loop.
- A loop that repeats infinite times is called an infinite loop.
- A loop counter is a variable that counts the number of iterations.
- Different loops have different application area though one loop can be converted to another.
- The do...while loop is applied in those cases where it is taken for granted that a task will take place at least once and then will repeat as long as a condition is true.
- **Comparison of the various loop statements**
    - **For Loop** : When the number of iterations and the changes in the loop counter is known, this loop is preferred. It is an entry controlled loop.
    - **While Loop** : When the change in loop counter is not known and the number of iterations is also not fixed, then while loop is used. It is an entry controlled loop.
    - **Do While Loop** : This loop is similar to while loop with the difference that its block gets executed at least once. Only this loop ends with a semicolon, at its end. It is an exit controlled loop.
- The break statement causes a loop to terminate its iterations. Whenever a break is encountered, the control comes out to the statement next to the block of the loop.
- The continue statement causes the loop to skip the rest of the statements for that round and go to the next round of iteration.
- Dummy loop is a loop that does not have any task in it. But an empty loop is not an infinite loop. One application area of empty loop is in "to wait or to delay".

SOLVED QUESTIONS

1. **What is a loop used for ?**
   Answer : A loop is used to perform repetitive tasks.
2. **What are the components of a loop ?**
   Answer : Every loop has the following components :

(i) Loop counter : A variable that counts the number of times a loop is repeating.

(ii) Initialization : The initial value of a loop counter.

(iii) Test Condition : The criteria that indicates whether the loop should repeat or not.

(iv) Updation : The modification of the loop counter.

3. **How is a while loop different from a do...while loop ?**

   Answer. While Loop : When the change in loop counter is not known and the number of iterations is also not fixed, then while loop is used. It is an entry controlled loop.

   Do While Loop : This loop is similar to while loop with the difference that its block gets executed at least once. It is the only loop that ends with a semicolon, at its end. It is an exit controlled loop.

4. **What is the use of a break statement ? Explain using an example.**

   Answer : The break statement causes a loop to terminate its iterations. Whenever a break is encountered, the control comes out to the statement next to the block of the loop.

   For example :

```
//break in for loop                    Output
for ( k = 10;  k <= 30 ; k= k + 4)
{                                       10    14   22
    System.out.print ( k + "  " );
    if ( k ==  22)
    {
        break;
    }
}
// break in while loop                 Output
int m = 25;                            25
while ( m <= 50)                       30
{                                      35
    if ( m > 40)                       40
    {
        break;
    }
        System.out.println (m);
        m = m + 5;
}
```

5. **What is the use of a 'continue' statement ? Explain using an example.**

   Answer : The continue statement causes the loop to skip the rest of the statements for that round and go to the next round of iteration.

	Output
```//continue in for loop```	
```for (k = 10; k <= 30 ; k= k + 4)```	
```{```	10 14 26 30
``` if (k = = 22)```	
``` {```	
``` continue ;```	
``` }```	
``` System.out.print (k + " ");```	
```}```	

	Output
```// continue in while loop```	
```int m = 25;```	25
```while (m <= 50)```	30
```{```	35
``` if (m > 40)```	40
``` {```	
``` continue;```	
``` }```	
``` System.out.println (m);```	
``` m = m + 5;```	
```}```	

6 **Given below are codes on 'for loops' those have some errors. Rewrite the codes after correcting the errors.**

(a) for (j = 0 j < 5 j++)

Answer : for (j = 0 ; j < 5 ; j++)

(b) for   p = 15 ; p<= 25 ; p++

Answer : for (p = 15; p <= 25 ; p++)

(c) for (q = 1 ; q <= 100 ; q = = q + 10)

Answer : for (q = 1 ; q <= 100 ; q = q + 10)

(d) for (s>= 5 ; s = 1 ; s - -)

Answer. for (s = 5 ; s >= 1 ; s - -)

(e) for (t = 20 , c <15 , c++)

Answer. for (t = 20 ; c > 15 ; c - -)

(f)   for (u = 6425 :   u > 0 : u = u / 10)

Answer. for (u = 6425 ;   u > 25 ; u = u / 10)

(g) for (w = 365 ; w > 0 ; w = w + 20)

Answer. for (w = 365 ; w > 0 ; w = w - 20)

7 **Given below are codes on 'while loops' that have some errors. Rewrite the codes after correcting the errors.**

(a) int g = 45;
     while (g > 35)
        {

```
            System.out.print( g + "   " );
    }
```

Answer.
```
int  g = 45;
    while ( g > 35 )
    {
        System.out.print( g + "   " );
        g - - ;
    }
```

(b)
```
int  h = 100;
while ( h > 0 )
{
    System.out.print( h + "   " ) ;
    h = h + 10 ;
}
```

Answer :
```
int h = 100;
    while ( h > 0 )
    {
        System.out.print( h + "   " ) ;
        h = h - 10 ;
    }
```

(c)
```
int j = 2048 ;
do
{
    System.out.print( j + "   " ) ;
    j = j / 2 ;
} while ( j> 2048 ) ;
```

Answer :
```
int j = 2048 ;
    do
    {
        System.out.print( j + "   " ) ;
        j = j / 2 ;
    }while ( j > 0 ) ;
```

EXERCISE

Question 1. Answer the following in brief :

(a) What is the function of a loop ?

(b) What is jump statement? What are the different types of Jump statements available in Java ?

(c) What is meant by an infinite loop ?

(d) What is the difference between a for loop and a while loop ?

(e) How is an exit controlled loop different from an entry controlled loop ?

Question 2. State true or false :

(a) A for loop uses separator comma (,) for its segments initialization, condition, increment.

(b) do...while loop is an entry controlled loop.

(c) Break statement terminates a loop.

(d) Continue statement terminates a loop.

(e) A while loop is always an infinite loop.

Question 3. Identify the error, if any, in the following code snippets :

(a) for [k = 0; k<10; k++]

(b) for (int m = 5; m > 1; m++)

(c) for { int g = 1; g<= 5 ; g++ }

(d) for (g = 1, h = 5 ; g<h ; g++, h--)

(e) for (c = 15, c < 20 , c++)

Question. 4. Given the codes, write the output with justification :

```
(a)  int h = 4;
     while ( h > 4)
     {
         System.out.println ( h );
         h++ ;
     }

(c)  int g = 15;
     while ( g == 15)
     {
         System.out.println ( g );
         g++ ;
     }
```

```
(b)  int y = 4;
     do
     {
         System.out.println ( y + "" );
         y++;
     }while ( y < 9);

(d)  int q = 25;
     do
     {
         System.out.println ( q );
         q-- ;
     }while ( q < 9) ;
```

Chapter 7

NESTED FOR LOOPS

Contents
- Introduction to Nested Loop through Simple Examples
- Rectangular Patterns
- Right Triangular Patterns
- Right Triangular Patterns with Leading Spaces
- Series involving single variable
- Application of break and continue

INTRODUCTION TO NESTED LOOP

We have seen so far that in a program, a code can be repeated many times using a loop. The body of a loop can contain any programming code. Now we will look at a nested loop.

In a nested loop structure, there exists a loop inside another loop. The code of the inner loop repeats with each iteration of the outer loop.

The following example of program code shows how nested loop works

```
for(r = 1; r <= 4; r++)
{
    for(c = 21; c <= 26; c++)
    {
        System.out.print("   " + c);
    }
    System.out.println ( );
}
```

Output of the above code :

```
21   22   23   24   25   26
21   22   23   24   25   26
21   22   23   24   25   26
21   22   23   24   25   26
```

Explanation :

- For each counter value of the outer loop, the inner loop gets executed. The inner loop starts afresh each time the outer loop repeats.
- The outer loop has loop counter **r** which is repeating from 1 to 4 (4 times).
- Inside its body, there exists the inner loop which has loop counter **c** which is repeating from 21 to 26 (6 times).
- The inner loop has a print statement without new line. It makes the printing happen in the same line.
- Each time the inner loop completes its iteration, a new line is printed.

Nested loops can be used to print various patterns. We will learn to make rectangular, right triangular patterns and series with single variable.

Let us now look at some more examples.

NESTED LOOP FOR RECTANGULAR PATTERNS

To make a rectangular pattern, the inner loop repeats a fixed number of times along with the outer loop. Observe the working of the given examples.

Example 1.

```java
import java.util.Scanner;
public class NestedLoop
{
    void main()
    {
        int r = 0, c = 0;
        for(r = 1; r <= 5; r++)
        {
            for(c = 100; c <= 500; c = c + 100)
            {
                System.out.print("   " + c);
            }
            System.out.println ( );
        }
    }
}
```

Output :   100   200   300   400   500
           100   200   300   400   500
           100   200   300   400   500
           100   200   300   400   500
           100   200   300   400   500

Explanation :

- The outer loop has loop counter **r** which is repeating from 1 to 5 (5 times).
- Inside its body, there exists the inner loop which has loop counter **c** which is repeating from 100 to 500 with a gap of 100 (5 times).

Example 2.

```java
import java.util.Scanner;
public class NestedLoop
{
    void main()
    {
        int r = 0, c = 0 ;
        for(r = 1; r <= 3; r++)
        {
            for(c = 25; c >= 5; c = c - 5)
            {
                System.out.print("   " + c);
            }
            System.out.println ( );
        }
    }
}
```

Output: 25 20 15 10 5

                      25 20 15 10 5

                      25 20 15 10 5

Explanation :

- The outer loop has loop counter **r** which is repeating from 1 to 3 (3 times).
- The inner loop has loop counter **c**, it is repeating from 25 down to 5 with a gap of 5 (5 times).

Example 3.

```java
import java.util.Scanner;
public class NestedLoop
{
    void main()
    {
        int r = 0, c = 0;
        for(r = 50; r >= 25; r = r - 5)
        {
            for(c = 1; c <= 10; c++)
            {
                System.out.print("   " + c);
            }
            System.out.println ( );
        }
    }
}
```

Output :   1 2 3 4 5 6 7 8 9 10
         1 2 3 4 5 6 7 8 9 10
         1 2 3 4 5 6 7 8 9 10
         1 2 3 4 5 6 7 8 9 10
         1 2 3 4 5 6 7 8 9 10
         1 2 3 4 5 6 7 8 9 10

Explanation :

- The outer loop has loop counter **r** which is repeating from 50 to 25 with a gap of 5(6 times).
- The inner loop has loop counter **c** , it is repeating from 1 to 10 (10 times).

Example 4.

```java
import java.util.Scanner;
public class NestedLoop
{
    void main()
    {
        int r = 0, c = 0 ;
        for(r = 5; r >= 1; r- -)
        {
            for(c = 1; c <= 6; c++)
            {
                System.out.print("   " + r);
            }
            System.out.println ( );
        }
    }
}
```

Output :   5 5 5 5 5 5
         4 4 4 4 4 4
         3 3 3 3 3 3
         2 2 2 2 2 2
         1 1 1 1 1 1

Explanation :

- This program is repeating the outer loop counter, which is **r**, from 5 to 1 (5 times) and printing it in the inner loop.
- The inner loop has loop counter **c** , it is repeating from 1 to 6 (6 times).
- This is the reason for each row to have the value of **r** getting printed 6 times.

Example 5.

```java
import java.util.Scanner;
public class NestedLoop
{
```

```
        void main()
        {
            int r = 0, c = 0 ;
            for(r = 1; r <= 6; r++ )
            {
                for(c = 1; c <= 7; c++)
                {
                    System.out.print("   **  " + r);
                }
                System.out.println ( );
            }
        }
```

Output :

```
** 1   ** 1   ** 1   ** 1   ** 1   ** 1   ** 1
** 2   ** 2   ** 2   ** 2   ** 2   ** 2   ** 2
** 3   ** 3   ** 3   ** 3   ** 3   ** 3   ** 3
** 4   ** 4   ** 4   ** 4   ** 4   ** 4   ** 4
** 5   ** 5   ** 5   ** 5   ** 5   ** 5   ** 5
** 6   ** 6   ** 6   ** 6   ** 6   ** 6   ** 6
```

Explanation :

- This program is repeating the outer loop counter, which is **r**, from 1 to 6 (6 times) and priting it in the inner loop.
- The inner loop has loop counter **c**, it is repeating from 1 to 7 (7 times).
- This is the reason for each row to have the value of **r** getting printed 7 times.

Example 6.

```
import java.util.Scanner;
public class NestedLoop
{
    void main()
    {
        int r = 0, c = 0 ;
        for(r = 50; r >= 25; r = r – 5)
        {
            for(c = 1; c <= 6; c++)
            {
                System.out.print("   " + r);
            }
            System.out.println ( );
        }
    }
}
```

Output :   50 50 50 50 50 50
                45 45 45 45 45 45
                40 40 40 40 40 40
                35 35 35 35 35 35
                30 30 30 30 30 30
                25 25 25 25 25 25

Explanation :

- This program is repeating the outer loop counter, which is **r**, from 50 to 25 (6 times) and printing it in the inner loop.
- The inner loop has loop counter **c**, it is repeating from 1 to 6 (6 times).
- This is the reason for each row to have the value of **r** getting printed 6 times.

Example 7.

```java
import java.util.Scanner;
public class NestedLoop
{
    void main()
    {
        int r = 0, c = 0;
        for(r = 4; r >= 1; r--)
        {
            for(c = 1; c <= 5; c++)
            {
                System.out.print(" * ");
            }
            System.out.println ( );
        }
    }
}
```

Output :   *   *   *   *   *
                *   *   *   *   *
                *   *   *   *   *
                *   *   *   *   *

Explanation :

- The outer loop counter **r** is repeating from 4 down to 1 (4 times).
- The inner loop counter **c**, is repeating from 1 to 5 (5 times).
- This is the reason for each row to print '*' 5 times

Example 8.

```java
import java.util.Scanner;
public class NestedLoop
{
    void main()
```

```java
    {
        int r = 0, c = 0;
        for(r = 9; r >= 1; r = r - 2)
        {
            System.out.print ( " R : " + r + " ## C : " );
            for(c = 60; c <= 80; c=c+5)
            {
                System.out.print("   " + c);
            }
            System.out.println ( );
        }
    }
}
```

Output :   R : 9 ## C :   60   65   70   75   80
                    R : 7 ## C :   60   65   70   75   80
                    R : 5 ## C :   60   65   70   75   80
                    R : 3 ## C :   60   65   70   75   80
                    R : 1 ## C :   60   65   70   75   80

Explanation :

- The outer loop counter **r** is repeating from 9 down to 1 with a gap of 2(5 times).
- The inner loop counter **c** , is repeating from 60 to 80 (5 times).
- The inner loop is only printing the value of **c** and the outer loop is printing the value of **r** along with some text and is also printing new line each time.

Example 9.

```java
import java.util.Scanner;
public class NestedLoop
{
    void main()
    {
        int r = 0, c = 0;
        for(r = 1; r <= 6; r++)
        {
            for(c = 5; c <= 9; c++)
            {
                System.out.print(" # " + c + " * ");
            }
            System.out.println ( );
        }
    }
}
```

Output :

```
#5   *#6   *#7   *#8   *#9*
#5   *#6   *#7   *#8   *#9*
#5   *#6   *#7   *#8   *#9*
#5   *#6   *#7   *#8   *#9*
#5   *#6   *#7   *#8   *#9*
#5   *#6   *#7   *#8   *#9*
```

Explanation :

- The outer loop counter **r** is repeating from 1 to 6 (6 times).
- The inner loop counter **c**, is repeating from 5 to 9 (5 times).
- The inner loop is printing the value of **c** along with some more symbols before and after it.

NESTED LOOP FOR RIGHT TRIANGULAR PATTERNS

Nested loops can be used for making right triangular patters. To do so, the inner loop is repeated for a varying number of times. Each time the outer loop repeats, the inner loop counter should get a different limit value.

Observe the working of the given examples.

Example 1.

```java
import java.util.Scanner;
public class NestedLoop
{
    void main()
    {
        int r = 0, c = 0;
        for ( r = 1; r <= 5; r++ )
        {
            for(c = 1; c <= r; c++)
            {
                System.out.print("   " + c);
            }
            System.out.println ( );
        }
    }
}
```

Output :

```
1
1  2
1  2  3
1  2  3  4
1  2  3  4  5
```

Explanation :

- The outer loop counter **r** is repeating from 1 to 5 (5 times).
- The inner loop counter **c**, is not repeating fixed number of time with each **r**. Its upper limit is changing with the outer loop counter **r**. So each time r changes, the iteration count of **c** also changes.

    When r = 1, range of c is from 1 to 1
    When r = 2, range of c is from 1 to 2
    When r = 3, range of c is from 1 to 3
    When r = 4, range of c is from 1 to 4
    When r = 5, range of c is from 1 to 5

Example 2.

```java
import java.util.Scanner;
public class NestedLoop
{
    void main()
    {
        int r = 0, c = 0;
        for ( r = 1; r <= 5; r++ )
        {
            for(c = 1; c <= r; c++)
            {
                System.out.print(" * ");
            }
            System.out.println ( );
        }
    }
}
```

Output :
```
*
*   *
*   *   *
*   *   *   *
*   *   *   *   *
```

Explanation :

- The outer loop counter **r** is repeating from 1 to 5 (5 times).
- The inner loop counter **c**, is not repeating fixed number of time with each **r**. Its upper limit is changing with the outer loop counter **r**. So each time r changes, the iteration count of **c** also changes.

    When r = 1, range of c is from 1 to 1, printing * 1 time
    When r = 2, range of c is from 1 to 2, printing * 2 times
    When r = 3, range of c is from 1 to 3, printing * 3 times
    When r = 4, range of c is from 1 to 4, printing * 4 times

When r = 5, range of c is from 1 to 5, printing * 5 times

Example 3.

```java
import ava.util.Scanner;
public class NestedLoop
{
    void main()
    {
        int r = 0, c = 0;
        for ( r = 1; r <= 5; r++ )
        {
            for(c = r; c <= 6; c++)
            {
                System.out.print("   " + c);
            }
            System.out.println ( );
        }
    }
}
```

Output :
```
1   2   3   4   5   6
2   3   4   5   6
3   4   5   6
4   5   6
5   6
```

Explanation :

- The outer loop counter **r** is repeating from 1 to 5 (5 times).
- The inner loop counter **c** has the following range ,
  When r = 1, range of c is from 1 to 6
  When r = 2, range of c is from 2 to 6
  When r = 3, range of c is from 3 to 6
  When r = 4, range of c is from 4 to 6
  When r = 5, range of c is from 5 to 6

Example 4.

```java
import java.util.Scanner;
public class NestedLoop
{
    void main()
    {
        int r = 0, c = 0;
        for ( r = 1; r <= 5; r++ )
        {
            for(c = r; c <= 5; c++)
```

```
            {
                System.out.print(" # ") ;
            }
            System.out.println ( ) ;
        }
    }
}
```

Output :
```
# # # # #
# # # #
# # #
# #
#
```

Explanation :

- The outer loop counter **r** is repeating from 1 to 5 (5 times).
- The inner loop counter **c** has the following range ,
  When r = 1, range of c is from 1 to 5, printing # 5 times
  When r = 2, range of c is from 2 to 5, printing # 4 times
  When r = 3, range of c is from 3 to 5, printing # 3 times
  When r = 4, range of c is from 4 to 5, printing # 2 times
  When r = 5, range of c is from 5 to 5, printing # 1 time

Example 5.

```
import java.util.Scanner;
public class NestedLoop
{
    void main()
    {
        int r = 0, c = 0;
        for ( r = 5; r >= 1; r-- )
        {
            for(c = r ; c >= 1; c--)
            {
                System.out.print("   " + c);
            }
            System.out.println ( );
        }
    }
}
```

Output :
```
5 4 3 2 1
4 3 2 1
3 2 1
2 1
1
```

- The outer loop counter **r** is repeating from 5 down to 1 (5 times).
- The inner loop counter **c** has the following range ,

  When r = 5, range of c is from 5 down to 1

  When r = 4, range of c is from 4 down to 1

  When r = 3, range of c is from 3 down to 1

  When r = 2, range of c is from 2 down to 1

  When r = 1, range of c is from 1 down to 1 (equal in this case)

Example 6.

```java
import java.util.Scanner;
public class NestedLoop
{
    void main()
    {
        int r = 0, c = 0;
        for ( r = 1; r <= 5; r++ )
        {
            for(c = r ; c >= 1; c--)
            {
                System.out.print("   " + c);
            }
            System.out.println ( );
        }
    }
}
```

Output: 1

          2 1

          3 2 1

          4 3 2 1

          5 4 3 2 1

- The outer loop counter **r** is repeating from 1 to 5 (5 times).
- The inner loop counter **c** has the following range ,

  When r = 1, range of c is from 1 down to 1 (equal in this case)

  When r = 2, range of c is from 2 down to 1

  When r = 3, range of c is from 3 down to 1

  When r = 4, range of c is from 4 down to 1

  When r = 5, range of c is from 5 down to 1

TRIANGULAR PATTERNS WITH LEADING SPACES

In the next section, let us look at some more triangular patters. In these patterns, in each row, there are two sets of columns. One set is for leading spaces (or symbols) and the other set is for following values (or symbols). These patterns are called patterns with leading spaces.

Example 7.

```java
import java.util.Scanner;
public class NestedLoop
{
    void main()
    {
        int r = 0, c = 0, d = 0 ;
        for(r = 1; r <= 5; r++)
        {
            for(c=1; c<= r; c++)
            {
                System.out.print(" ."); // to print leading dots in each row, 2 space &
                1 dot
            }
            for( d = r; d <= 5; d++)
            {
                System.out.print("  " + d); // to print digits each row, 2 space & 1
                number
            }
            System.out.println ( );
        }
    }
}
```

Output :

```
   .  1  2  3  4  5
   .  .  2  3  4  5
   .  .  .  3  4  5
   .  .  .  .  4  5
   .  .  .  .  .  5
```

Explanation :

- The outer loop counter **r** is repeating from 1 to 5 (5 times).
- There are two inner loops, one is with loop counter **c** and the other is with loop counter **d**
- In each row, the 1st inner loop (with loop counter c) prints the dots and immediately after that the 2nd inner loop (with loop counter d) prints the numbers.

Hence the output appears as -

When r = 1, range of c is from 1 to 1, printing 1 dot

               range of d is from 1 to 5, printing 5 numbers from 1 to 5

When r = 2, range of c is from 1 to 2, printing 2 dots

               range of d is from 2 to 5, printing 4 numbers from 2 to 5

When r = 3, range of c is from 1 to 3, printing 3 dots
            range of d is from 3 to 5, printing 3 numbers from 3 to 5
When r = 4, range of c is from 1 to 4, printing 4 dots
            range of d is from 4 to 5, printing 2 numbers from 4 to 5
When r = 5, range of c is from 1 to 5, printing 5 dots
            range of d is from 5 to 5, printing 1 number from 5 to 5

Example 8.

```java
import java.util.Scanner;
public class NestedLoop
{
    void main()
    {
        int r = 0, c = 0, d = 0;
        for(r = 5; r >= 1; r- - )
        {
            for(c=1; c<= r; c++)
            {
                System.out.print(" ."); // to print leading dots in each row, 2 space &
                1 dot
            }
            for( d = r; d <= 5; d++)
            {
                System.out.print("  " + d); // to print digits each row, 2 space & 1
                number
            }
            System.out.println ( );
        }
    }
}
```

Output :   5
                   4   5
                 . .   .   3   4   5
                 . .   2   3   4   5
                 . 1   2   3   4   5

Explanation :

- The outer loop counter **r** is repeating from 5 down to 1(5 times).
- There are two inner loops, one is with loop counter **c** and the other is with loop counter **d**
- In each row, the 1st inner loop (with loop counter c) prints the dots and immediately after that the 2nd inner loop (with loop counter d) prints the numbers.

Hence the output appears as -

When r = 5, range of c is from 1 to 5, printing 5 dots
            range of d is from 5 to 5, printing 1 number from 5 to 5

When r = 4, range of c is from 1 to 4, printing 4 dots
        range of d is from 4 to 5, printing 2 numbers from 4 to 5
When r = 3, range of c is from 1 to 3, printing 3 dots
        range of d is from 3 to 5, printing 3 numbers from 3 to 5
When r = 2, range of c is from 1 to 2, printing 2 dots
        range of d is from 2 to 5, printing 4 numbers from 2 to 5
When r = 1, range of c is from 1 to 1, printing 1 dot
        range of d is from 1 to 5, printing 5 number from 1 to 5

Example 9.

```java
import java.util.Scanner;
public class NestedLoop
{
    void main()
    {
        int r = 0, c = 0, d = 0;
        for(r = 5; r >= 1; r--)
        {
            for(c=1; c<= r; c++)
            {
                System.out.print("  "); // to print leading spaces
            }
            for(d = r; d <= 5; d++)
            {
                System.out.print(" *");
            }
            System.out.println ( ) ;
        }
    }
}
```

Output :

```
                *
            *   *
        *   *   *
    *   *   *   *
*   *   *   *   *
```

Explanation :

- The outer loop counts the number of rows, loop counter r (5 in this case).
- For each value of r, at first spaces are printed and then symbol * is printed. The working is similar as above.

SERIES INVOLVING SINGLE VARIABLE

In this section, we look in simple operation on series using nested loop. The outer loop controls how many times the inner loop will get activated.

Example 1. Find the Summation of each number from 1 to 5 and print the result each time.

```
import java.util.Scanner;
public class NestedLoop
{
    void main()
    {
        int r = 0, c = 0, sum = 0 ;
        for ( r = 1; r <= 5; r++ )
        {
            for(c = 1; c <= r; c++)
            {
                sum = sum + c;
            }
            System.out.println(" At r = " + r  + " SUMMATION = " + sum );
            sum = 0;
        }
    }
}
```

Output :   At r = 1 SUMMATION = 1
             At r = 2 SUMMATION = 3
             At r = 3 SUMMATION = 6
             At r = 4 SUMMATION = 10
             At r = 5 SUMMATION = 15

Explanation : As per the question, Summation of each number from 1 to 5 has been asked.

- The variable **sum** works as an accumulator and stores the result each time.
- The inner loop calculates the sum each time.
- The result is printed and the accumulator **sum** is cleared each time before updating the loop counter **r**

Note 1 :

If sum is not cleared then there will be an error in the calculation of the following cases.

Example 2. Find the Factorial of each number from 4 to 7 and print the result each time.

[Factorial of number n is product of all numbers from 1 to n]

```
import java.util.Scanner;
public class NestedLoop
{
    void main()
    {
```

```java
        int r = 0, c = 0, p = 1;
        for ( r = 4; r <= 7; r++ )
        {
            for(c = 1; c <= r; c++)
            {
                p = p* c ;
            }
            System.out.println( " At r = " + r  + " FACTORIAL = " + p );
            p = 1;
        }
    }
}
```

Output :   At r = 4 FACTORIAL = 24
                  At r = 5 FACTORIAL = 120
                  At r = 6 FACTORIAL = 720
                  At r = 7 FACTORIAL = 5040

Explanation : As per the question, Factorial of each number from 4 to 7 has been asked.

- The variable **p** works as an accumulator and stores the result each time.
- The inner loop calculates the product each time.
- The result is printed and the accumulator **p** is cleared by making it 1 each time before updating the loop counter **r**

Note 1 :

If p is not made 1 then the result of product will give error.

Example 3. Find the Summation of even numbers from 2 to 10 and print the result each time.

```java
import java.util.Scanner;
public class NestedLoop
{
    void main()
    {
        int r = 0, c = 0, sum = 0 ;
        for ( r = 2; r <= 10; r = r + 2 )
        {
            for(c = 1; c <= r; c++)
            {
                sum = sum + c ;
            }
            System.out.println( " At r = " + r  + " SUMMATION = " + sum ) ;
            sum = 0 ;
        }
    }
}
```

Output : At r = 2 SUMMATION = 3
At r = 4 SUMMATION = 10
At r = 6 SUMMATION = 21
At r = 8 SUMMATION = 36
At r = 10 SUMMATION = 55

Explanation : As per the question, Summation of even numbers from 2 to 10 has been asked.

- The variable **sum** works as an accumulator and stores the result each time.
- The inner loop calculates the sum each time.
- The result is printed and the accumulator **sum** is cleared each time before updating the loop counter **r**

Note 1 :

If sum is not cleared then there will be error in calculation of following cases.

Example 4. Print the multiples of numbers from 10 to 14, from 1 to 10 for each.

```java
import java.util.Scanner;
public class NestedLoop
{
    void main()
    {
        int r = 0, c = 0, M = 0 ;
        for ( r = 10; r <= 14; r++ )
        {
            System.out.print( " Multiples of " + r + " :: " ) ;
            for(c = 1; c <= 10; c++)
            {
                M = r * c ;
                System.out.print( "   " + M );
            }
            System.out.println ( );
        }
    }
}
```

Output : Multiples of 10 :: 10 20 30 40 50 60 70 80 90 100
Multiples of 11 :: 11 22 33 44 55 66 77 88 99 110
Multiples of 12 :: 12 24 36 48 60 72 84 96 108 120
Multiples of 13 :: 13 26 39 52 65 78 91 104 117 130
Multiples of 14 :: 14 28 42 56 70 84 98 112 126 140

Explanation :

As per the question, Multiples of each number from 10 to 14 has been asked.

- The variable M stores the result each time. Since it is not an accumulator (reinitializing itself), it is not compulsory to clear it.
- The inner loop calculates the product each time and prints it.

APPLICATION OF BREAK AND CONTINUE IN NESTED LOOP

In a loop, statement *break* is used for terminating the iterations. In case of nested loop, break statement terminates the immediate loop it is in.

Similarly, statement continue is used for going to next iteration by deserting the remaining statements of the current iteration. In case of nested loop, continue statement works for the immediate loop it is in.

The following examples demonstrate the above concepts.

Example 1.

```java
import java.util.Scanner;
public class NestedLoop
{
    void main()
    {
        for ( int r = 1; r <= 6; r++ )
        {
            System.out.print (" R = " + r );
            for(int c = 1; c <= 10; c++)
            {
                if ( c == 6)
                {
                    break ;
                }
                System.out.print( "  " + c );
            }
            System.out.println ( );
        }
    }
}
```

Output :   R = 1 1 2 3 4 5
                 R = 2 1 2 3 4 5
                 R = 3 1 2 3 4 5
                 R = 4 1 2 3 4 5
                 R = 5 1 2 3 4 5
                 R = 6 1 2 3 4 5

Explanation :

- In the above program, each time **c == 6** , the loop of **c** (the inner loop) terminates due to the **break** statement.

Example 2.

```java
import java.util.Scanner;
public class NestedLoop
{
    void main()
    {
        for ( int r = 1; r <= 6; r++ )
        {
            System.out.print (" R = " + r );
            for(int c = 1; c <= 10; c++)
            {
                if ( r == 4)
                {
                    break ;
                }
                System.out.print( "   " + c );
            }
            System.out.println ( );
        }
    }
}
```

Output :   R = 1 1 2 3 4 5 6 7 8 9 10
                 R = 2 1 2 3 4 5 6 7 8 9 10
                 R = 3 1 2 3 4 5 6 7 8 9 10
                 R = 4
                 R = 5 1 2 3 4 5 6 7 8 9 10
                 R = 6 1 2 3 4 5 6 7 8 9 10

Explanation :

In the above program, when **r == 4**, the loop of **c** (the inner loop) misses one full set of values from 1 to 10. Then when again **r** becomes 5, it starts working.

- -

Example 3.

```java
import java.util.Scanner;
public class NestedLoop
{
    void main()
    {
        for ( int r = 1; r <= 6; r++ )
        {
            System.out.print (" R = " + r );
            for(int c = 1; c <= 10; c++)
            {
```

```
            if ( c == 7)
            {
                System.out.print( "  $$ " );
                continue ;
            }
            System.out.print( "  " + c );
        }
        System.out.println ( );
    }
  }
}
```

Output :   R = 1 1 2 3 4 5 6 $$ 8 9 10
          R = 2 1 2 3 4 5 6 $$ 8 9 10
          R = 3 1 2 3 4 5 6 $$ 8 9 10
          R = 4 1 2 3 4 5 6 $$ 8 9 10
          R = 5 1 2 3 4 5 6 $$ 8 9 10
          R = 6 1 2 3 4 5 6 $$ 8 9 10

Explanation :

* In the above program, when c == 7, the loop of c (the inner loop) misses the statement that appears after **continue.**

Example 4.

```
import java.util.Scanner;
public class NestedLoop
{
    void main()
    {
        for ( int r = 1; r <= 6; r++ )
        {
            System.out.print (" R = " + r );
            for(int c = 1; c <= 10; c++)
            {
                if ( r == 3)
                {
                    System.out.print( "  ^" );
                    continue ;
                }
                System.out.print( "  " + c );
            }
            System.out.println ( );
```

```
            }
        }
    }
```

Output :   R = 1 1 2 3 4 5 6 7 8 9 10
              R = 2 1 2 3 4 5 6 7 8 9 10
              R = 3 ^ ^ ^ ^ ^ ^ ^ ^ ^ ^
              R = 4 1 2 3 4 5 6 7 8 9 10
              R = 5 1 2 3 4 5 6 7 8 9 10
              R = 6 1 2 3 4 5 6 7 8 9 10

Explanation :

- In the above program, when $r == 3$, the loop of **c** (the inner loop) applies statement **continue** on a full set of values from 1 to 10. Then when again **r** becomes 4, it starts working.

USE OF LABELS IN NESTED LOOP

A label is a text that is followed by a colon symbol (:). It helps in handling nested loop in one go.

When a label is given in front of a nested loop, the break or continue statement can be applied on the outer loop as well.

Observe the following examples :

Example 1.

```java
import java.util.Scanner;
public class NestedLoop
{
    void main()
    {
        Label1:
        for ( int r = 1; r <= 6; r++ )
        {
            System.out.print (" R = " + r );
            for(int c = 1; c <= 10; c++)
            {
                if ( c == 5)
                {
                    System.out.print ("Break with Label1  at c = 5.");
                    break Label1;
                }
                System.out.print( "   " + c );
            }
        }
```

```
            System.out.println ( );
         }
      }
   }
```

Output :   R = 1 1 2 3 4 Break with Label1 at c = 5.

Explanation :

Statement   *break Label1* is causing the outer loop to terminate as soon as the value of c == 5.

Example 2.

```
import java.util.Scanner;
public class NestedLoop
{
   void main()
   {
      Label1:
      for ( int r = 1; r <= 6; r++ )
      {
         System.out.print ("\n  R = " + r );
         for(int c = 1; c <= 10; c++)
         {
            if ( c == 3)
            {
               System.out.print ("Continue with Label1  at c = 3.");
               continue Label1;
            }
            System.out.print( "   " + c );
         }
         System.out.println ( );
      }
   }
}
```

Output :   R = 1 1 2 Continue with Label1 at c = 3.
              R = 2 1 2 Continue with Label1 at c = 3.
              R = 3 1 2 Continue with Label1 at c = 3.
              R = 4 1 2 Continue with Label1 at c = 3.
              R = 5 1 2 Continue with Label1 at c = 3.
              R = 6 1 2 Continue with Label1 at c = 3.

Explanation :

Each time c ==3, Statement *continue Label1* is causing the outer loop (r) to go to its next iteration.

SUMMARY

- In a nested loop structure, there exists a loop inside another loop.
- To make a rectangular pattern, the inner loop repeats a fixed number of times along with the outer loop.
- In a loop, statement *break* is used for terminating the iterations.
- In case of nested loop, break statement terminates the immediate loop it is in.
- Continue is used for going to next iteration by deserting the remaining statements of the current iteration.
- In case of nested loop, continue statement works for the immediate loop it is in.
- When a label is given in front of a nested loop, the break or continue statement can be applied on the outer loop as well.

EXERCISE

Question 1. Write a program to print the following patterns using nested for loops:

```
(a) 1 2 3 4 5 6 7
    1 2 3 4 5 6
    1 2 3 4 5
    1 2 3 4
    1 2 3
    1 2
    1
(b) 1
    1 2
    1 2 3
    1 2 3 4
    1 2 3 4 5
    1 2 3 4 5 6
    1 2 3 4 5 6 7
(c) 1 2 3 4 5 6 7
      2 3 4 5 6 7
        3 4 5 6 7
          4 5 6 7
            5 6 7
(d)           1
            1 2
          1 2 3
        1 2 3 4
      1 2 3 4 5
```

(e)
```
                9
              8 9
            7 8 9
          6 7 8 9
        5 6 7 8 9
```


Question 2. Given below is a pattern and a code with error. Rectify the code to produce the given output :

(a)
```
1
2 1
3 2 1
4 3 2 1
5 4 3 2 1
void main()
{
    int r = 0, c = 0;
    for ( r = 1; r <= 8; r++ )
    {
        for(c = r ; c >= 1; c+=2)
        {
            System.out.print("   " + c);
        }
        System.out.print ( );
    }
}
```

(b)
```
50  50  50  50  50  50
45  45  45  45  45  45
40  40  40  40  40  40
35  35  35  35  35  35
30  30  30  30  30  30
25  25  25  25  25  25
void main()
{
    int r = 0, c = 0 ;
    for ( r = 40; r >= 25; r = r + 5 )
    {
        for(c = 1; c <= 4; c++)
        {
            System.out.println("   " + r);
        }
        System.out.println ( );
    }
}
```

Question 3. Given below is a pattern and a partial code to make it. Complete the code to produce the given output.

(a)
```
# 5*   # 6 *   # 7 *   # 8 *   # 9*
# 5 *  # 6 *   # 7*    # 8 *   # 9*
# 5 *  # 6 *   # 7 *   # 8 *   # 9 *
# 5 *  # 6 *   # 7 *   # 8 *   # 9 *
# 5 *  # 6 *   # 7 *   # 8 *   # 9 *
# 5 *  # 6 *   # 7 *   # 8 *   # 9 *
```

```java
import java.util.Scanner;
public class NestedLoop
{
    void main()
    {
        int r = _, c = 0 ;
        for(r = _; r __ 6; r__)
        {
            for(c = __; c <= 9; c++)
            {
                System.out.print(" # " + c + " * ");
            }
            System.out.println ( );
        }
    }
}
```

(b)
```
*   *   *   *   *
*   *   *   *
*   *   *
*   *
*
```

```java
class Star
{
    void main()
    {
        int i, j;
        for(_=5;_>=_;_--)
        {
            for(j=1;j<=_;j++)
            {
                System.out.print("*");
            }
            System.out.println();
```

```
            }
        }
    }
(c) #   #   #   #   #
    #   #   #   #
    #   #   #
    #   #
    #
    public class NestedLoop
    {
        void main()
        {
            int r = 0, c = 0;
            for ( r = __; r __ 5; r__ )
            {
                for(__ = r; c __ 5; c++)
                {
                    System.out.print(" # ");
                }
                System.out._____ ( );
            }
        }
    }
```

(d) How many rows you want in this pattern?

```
7
Here is your pattern....!!!
1   2   3   4   5   6   7
1   2   3   4   5   6
1   2   3   4   5
1   2   3   4
1   2   3
1   2
1
import java.util.Scanner;
class Pattern
{
    void main()
    {
        Scanner sc = new Scanner(System.in);
        System.out.println("How many rows you want in this pattern?");
        int rows = sc.nextInt();
        System.out.println("Here is your pattern....!!!");
```

```java
        for (int i = ___; i >= 1; i--)
        {
            for (int __ = 1; j <= __; j__)
            {
                System.out.print(j+" ");
            }
            System.out.println();
        }
    }
}
```

Chapter 8

COMPUTING AND ETHICS

Contents
- Introduction
- Ethical Issues Related to Computing
- Intellectual Property Rights
- Protection of Individual's Right to Privacy
- Data Protection on the Internet
- Spam
- Software piracy
  - ❖ Types of software piracy
- Cyber Crime
  - ❖ Hacking
  - ❖ Phishing
  - ❖ Virus
- Protective Measures
  - ❖ Remaining Safe Online
- Netiquettes
- E-mail Etiquettes
- Summary
- Solved Questions
- Exercise

INTRODUCTION

The idea of computer ethics originated in the year 1950 when a book named, "The Human Use of Human Beings" by Norbert Weiner was published. A visionary mathematician and Philosopher, Norbert Weiner is also known as the father of computer ethics. In mid 20th century, the development of Information Technology started bringing in innumerous benefits. At the same time, it also started bringing in a lot of complications.

The temptation of gaining monetary profits or spreading rumors or distorting a news/image etc. became very difficult to overcome by the huge community of computer users. The society started having innocent victims for no good reason.

Computer ethics refer to the moral principles and the behavior of individuals working on computers.

Computer ethics also deals with matters regarding how computer professionals should behave while making decisions regarding professional as well as social conduct. It refers to the moral principles that monitor the use of computers.

In this chapter, we will be discussing various issues related to computer ethics and how data should be protected on the internet and on your computer.

ETHICAL ISSUES RELATED TO COMPUTING

The development of Information Technology today has led to many new inventions and innovations, which have made our life easier and flexible. However, even with these advantages, one has to deal with several social and ethical problems as a computer user. Ethical issues in computing may refer to making decisions about what's right and what's wrong and about how one's actions might affect others while working with computer technology. These issues may include protecting private and confidential data, protecting intellectual property of an individual and behaving responsibly.

Some of the major ethical issues associated with the availability and usage of information are discussed in this chapter.

INTELLECTUAL PROPERTY RIGHTS

Intellectual property refers to any intangible property that consists of original ideas and human knowledge. A lot of effort goes into the creation and generation of information and original ideas. Besides effort, an individual will have to put in time as well as money for developing original information and ideas. However, there are many people today who copy such information and use it for their own benefit. Copying does not require any effort as is required when it comes to creating original content.

> **REMEMBER**
>
> *Intellectual property is a person's creation which is not in material form.*

Examples are musical notes, strategies, ideas, literary pieces etc. Computer Software can also be considered as an Intellectual property.

Fig. 8.1

The true owner of such information must have the right to protect his/her intellectual property from being used by others. There are certain Laws and Rights that guard Intellectual properties. Listed below are the major Intellectual property rights.

(i) **Copyright :** It gives the right to the creator that no one can copy the same. However, someone can do the whole thing from the beginning keeping the basic idea same. Copyrighted items have a symbol of ©.

(ii) **Patent :** It protects an "idea". No one can work on a patented idea even if the whole plan is new.

(iii) **Trademark :** It is a distinct name that is used for some kind of goods or services. Symbol of trademark is ®.

(iv) **Trade Secrets :** These are certain formula or plan that is kept confidential for keeping the uniqueness of an item/property.

PROTECTION OF INDIVIDUAL'S RIGHT TO PRIVACY

An individual's right to privacy in the computing world refers to the following three issues :

- Collection of Information
- Storage of Information
- Distribution of Information

Privacy is a fundamental human right recognized by the United Nations. A person decides how much of his private life and thoughts he wants to reveal and share.

REMEMBER

The right to privacy suggests that the use of computers to collect, store and distribute data and information which belongs to someone else is unethical as it violates one's privacy.

Invading a person's privacy is a social crime. Hacking is a form of breaking an individual's right to privacy.

Fig. 8.2

In social networking sites, special care is taken on privacy rights. Actions are taken against that user who load images or write text that is objectionable by anyone.

DATA PROTECTION ON THE INTERNET

Today, a large number of people use the internet to conduct transactions worldwide. Such transactions and other communication involve the usage of sensitive and confidential information such as personal details, financial information, credit card, PIN numbers etc. With so much confidential information coursing through the internet, it is crucial that you take measures to safeguard your data when carrying out online transactions.

The Data Protection Act (DPA) protects the privacy and integrity of the data held on individuals by businesses and other organizations. Only authorized people can change/update data of individuals. No objectionable data/comment should be present for individuals.

SPAM

These are bulk e-mails that are sent to people generally for advertising, phishing etc. In some cases, spam may consume a lot of memory space.

Spams are unwanted e-mails sent from unknown people. To protect your mailbox and computer system from spams, mark the suspicious e-mails as spams, so that they will get deposited separately. Delete them later or you can use some filters, these filters come as special software packages which filter e-mails and discard unsuitable ones.

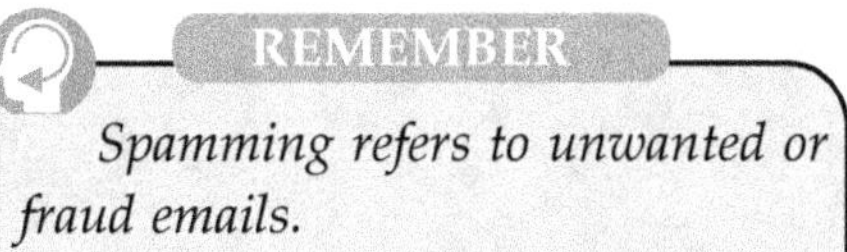

Fig. 8.3

SOFTWARE PIRACY

Software piracy refers to the unauthorized duplication of software. By buying any software, a person does not become the owner of that software. He only becomes a licensed user of that software and does not get the right to sell/give his copy to others.

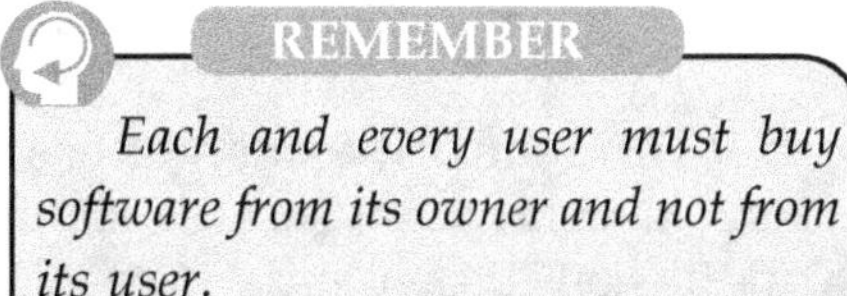

When we create copies of software and distribute it to our friends, we are actually promoting software piracy. Software piracy is a crime and as responsible computer users, we should not be a part of it.

Fig. 8.4

The actual act of software piracy involves using software in any illegal manner such as copying, downloading, sharing, selling etc. When you purchase software, what you are actually purchasing is the license to use it. It is just an authorized copy of that software. Besides that, you can reinstall that software on your system for only a specific number of times. If you try to extend that limit and make more copies of it, you are involved in software piracy.

Types of software piracy

Softlifting : Softlifting is one of the most common types of piracy. It refers to purchasing a single copy of software and sharing it with someone who is not authorized as a user under the license agreement.

Hard Disk Loading : This form of software piracy often involves hardware dealers. These dealers install unauthorized copies of software on the hard disk in order to get more customers to purchase hardware from them. This is how most operating systems, like Windows are often pirated.

Renting : Renting refers to giving away a copy of software to some other person for temporary use in exchange for a fee.

Uploading and Downloading : This refers to uploading unauthorized duplicates of licensed and copyrighted software online for general public usage. Any user connected to internet can be a part of such piracy.

Measures Against Software Piracy

There are certain measures one can take in order to control software piracy. This would include **copyrights, patents and trademark.**

Harms caused by Software Piracy

Software piracy is unethical. Some of the harms caused are :

- Financial loss to the creative programmers, who make them.
- Causes hike in the general cost of the Software.
- Programmers lose interest in making new creative software fearing the loss caused by piracy.
- Companies suffer financial loss as people purchase pirated software in place of the original software.

CYBER CRIME

It is true that the internet has many advantages but it also has many risk factors if proper care is not taken. One should not get carried away in temptation or greed while working on the internet. People with criminal intentions try various ways to trap innocent people or children. Some of the cyber crimes are hacking, piracy, organized child-trafficking, phishing, duping etc.

REMEMBER

Cyber crime refers to any crime, which involves the use of computers and networks.

Fig. 8.5

Hacking

It is an unethical act of breaking into the private zone of any user without the owner's permission. Hackers are those people who hack into people's personal information and use them for many wrong intensions such as frauds, etc.

Basically, hackers are people who know a lot about how computers, networks and programs work and have the ability to break into or bypass security and access the computer network usually for making profit. Sometimes hackers hack for fun and entertainment.

For example, a person accesses your e-mail id's password through unknown resources, to get your important files that are saved in your e-mail and are restricted to be disclosed with anyone, accessing your password without your permission is known as hacking.

Fig. 8.6

Phishing

It is the act of extracting important information from innocent users, by posing as someone reliable. Some websites carry out phishing by disguising themselves as any socially important website and then asking people to provide confidential information. This confidential information is later used for harmful purposes.

Fig. 8.7

Virus

These are harmful computer programs that cause damage to the information stored in the computer memory. They can hide themselves but can be felt when the computer shows unpredictable behavior. They get transmitted during data exchange with infected computer or while working online.

Computer virus refers to various malicious programs that hinder the system's performance.

Fig. 8.8

Some of the computer viruses are capable of deleting the entire files on the system. Viruses attached to any document or file will eventually spread all over the computer system. Example: Brain and Melissa virus, Bobbit virus, Ross Perot, Ollie North, Storm Worm, etc.

Worms : A worm is responsible for memory or disk crashes. Worms work by replicating themselves on the disk and taking up memory space until eventually the disk crashes. **Example:** I Love You, Morris, Sobig, Mydoom worm, etc.

Adware : Adware refers to the pop ups that open automatically on the system. They usually halt the current program and appear right in the center of the screen besides hogging your network bandwidth. **Example:** Some time advertising banners are downloaded automatically while installing some application from the internet.

Trojan Horse : Trojan horse refers to programs responsible for deleting and damaging files stored on the system. What makes them more dangerous is that they appear completely harmless.

Malware : Malware are basically malicious codes, designed to collect private and confidential data by gaining unauthorized access to resources of the system.

Sweeper : Sweeper is responsible for erasing all the files and folders on the system.

Password guessing : Password guessing is the mechanism used by hackers on the internet to retrieve user account passwords, which can then be misused for the hacker's benefits.

PROTECTIVE MEASURES

Now, that we have discussed various types of attacks, it's time to learn about what protective measures one can take in order to safeguard your system against such attacks.

(i) **Authentication** is the process of protecting important and confidential data on the computer system using login Id and password.

(ii) **Authorization** refers to the process of protecting inappropriate access to resources on the computer system.

(iii) **Accounting** refers to the tracking of network resources for the purpose of analysis, allocation and review. Tracking can be based on recording events such as the number of times an invalid password is entered by the user, or authentication and authorization failure, etc.

Fig. 8.9

(v) **Confidentiality** refers to the protection of information from access by unauthorized users. For instance, online shopping requires credit card number to be entered by the user which is highly confidential thus, **confidentiality** is used in order to protect such important information, number and other such data.

Remaining Safe Online

Recent news reveals that the internet has also become home of many illegal and unethical acts. Hence, it has become all the more necessary to remain safe while working on the internet. Given below are a few tips to remain safe on the internet.

(i) Change sensitive information (passwords) frequently : You must change your password at regular intervals so that nobody can crack your password. Cracking requires a number of repeated attempts, so if you change passwords regularly, it significantly reduces cracking threats.

(ii) Implement good surfing habits : Surfing illegal or bad sites may lead to problems with your system. To help reduce threats arising from browsing, one must pay careful attention while downloading and use secure browsers.

Fig. 8.10

(iii) Do not reveal your personal information: The Internet is constantly being used by millions of people all over the world. Revealing personal information to unknown people or unreliable websites may lead to stealing of data by cyber criminals. This may result in monetary loss or other harmful consequences.

(iv) Children must have parental supervision: Children have very high risk of falling victim to illegal sites. Bullying from harmful sites may lead to psychological disorders.

Fig. 8.11

(v) Sign off: After working on the internet in public computers, remember to remove your traces. In case you forget to sign off, any stranger can get access to your personal information and can also change your sensitive information and can make it inaccessible to you.

NETIQUETTES

Etiquette to be followed while using the Internet, is called **Netiquette**.

With the Internet proving so very useful to us, we should also be careful and sincere, while using it from our end. Ignorant or careless attitude may prove harmful to the society and can cause unnecessary trouble to millions of users who use the Internet.

What we Should Not Do :

(i) We should not use the computer to harm other people in any way.

(ii) We should not interfere with other people's work.

(iii) We should not disturb someone who is working over something important on the computer.

(iv) We should not spread wrong or harmful messages through the Internet.

(v) We should not go to those Websites for which we do not have permission.

What we Should Do :

(i) We should be helpful to people who are learning.

(ii) We should always use proper language and correct information in our messages.

(iii) We should always write messages with proper subject so that if the receiver is busy, he can decide whether he should give immediate attention to our message or can read it later.

(iv) We should be proud of our own culture and should respect cultures from all over the world as well. It will help in developing a beautiful relationship with people from all over the world through the Internet.

(v) We should stop our friends from doing wrong things on the computer.

E-MAIL ETIQUETTES

Etiquette means good manners. As a responsible citizen, one should maintain certain e-mail etiquettes.

A person Should Not

(i)   ask other's e-mail password.

(ii) open/read other's e-mail account.

(iii) forward gossips/false news via e-mail.

(iv) forward meaningless mails to others.

(v)   send mails without subject as without it the receiver cannot know its importance.

A person Should

(i)   help new users

(ii) use bcc in case a mail has to be sent/forwarded to various people.

(iii) remove the chain of addresses in case of multiple forwarding.

(iv) send/reply a formal letter by maintaining standards.

(v)   remember that alphabets in Upper Case indicates loudly spoken words. Avoid uppercase if not necessary.

SUMMARY

- Computer ethics refer to the moral principles and the behavior of individuals working on Computers.
- Ethical issues related to computing deal with several social and ethical problems as a computer user.
- Intellectual property refers to any intangible property that consists of original ideas and human knowledge. Examples are musical notes, strategies, ideas, etc
- Major Intellectual property rights are

  (i) Copyright   (ii) Patent   (iii) Trademark   (iv) Trade Secrets
- Protection of individual's right to privacy refers to the following three issues :
  - Collection of Information
  - Storage of Information
  - Distribution of Information
- Privacy is a fundamental human right recognized by the United Nations.
- Invading a person's privacy is a social crime. Hacking is a form of breaking individual's right to privacy.
- The Data Protection Act (DPA) protects the privacy and integrity of data held on individuals by businesses and other organizations. Only authorized people can change/update data of individuals.
- Spamming refers to unwanted or fraud e-mails.
- Software piracy refers to the unauthorized duplication of software. Its types are

  (i) Softlifting, (ii) Hard Disk Loading, (iii) Renting, (iv) Uploading and Downloading.
- Measures against Software Piracy include copyrights, patents and trademark.

- Cyber crime refers to any crime, which involves the use of computers and networks
- Hackers are those people who hack into people's personal information and use them for many wrong intensions.
- Phishing is the act of extracting important information from innocent users, by posing as someone reliable and misusing that information later.
- Computer virus refers to various malicious programs that hinder the system's performance.
- Worms work by replicating itself on the disk and taking up memory space until eventually the disk crashes.
- Adware refers to the pop ups that open automatically on the system.
- Trojan horse refers to programs responsible for deleting and damaging files stored on the system.
- Malware are basically malicious codes, designed to collect private and confidential data by gaining unauthorized access to resources of the system.
- To safeguard your system against such attacks, apply preventive measures such as Authentication, Authorization, Accounting and Confidentiality
- Etiquette to be followed while using the Internet, is called **Netiquette**.

SOLVED QUESTIONS

1. **What are computer Ethics ?**

   Answer : Computer ethics refer to the moral principles and the behavior of individuals working on Computers.

2. **Explain the following terms :**

(i) **Worms**	(ii) **Sweeper**	(iii) **Trojan Horse**
(iv) **Phishing**	(v) **Adware**	

   Answer :

   (i) **Worms :** A worm is responsible for memory or disk crashes. Worms work by replicating itself on the disk and taking up memory space until eventually the disk crashes.

   (ii) **Sweeper :** Sweeper is responsible for erasing all the files and folders on the system.

   (iii) **Trojan Horse :** Trojan horse refers to programs responsible for deleting and damaging files stored on the system. What makes them more dangerous is that they appear completely harmless

   (iv) **Phishing :** It is the act of extracting important information from innocent users, by posing as someone reliable. The confidential information are later used for harmful purposes.

   (v) **Adware :** Adware refers to the pop ups that open automatically on the system. They usually halt the current program and appear right in the center of the screen besides hogging your network bandwidth.

3. **What are the harms caused by piracy ?**

   Answer : Software piracy is unethical. Some of the harms caused are :
   - Financial loss to the creative programmers, who make them.
   - Causes hike in the general cost of the software.
   - Programmers loose interest in making new creative software fearing the loss caused by piracy.
   - Companies suffer financial loss as people purchase pirated software in place of the original software.

4. **What are the types of software piracy ?**

   Answer :

   Softlifting : It refers to purchasing a single copy of software and sharing it with someone who is not authorized as a user under the license agreement.

   Hard Disk Loading: This form of software piracy often involves hardware dealers. The dealers install unauthorized copies of software on the hard disk in order to get more customers.

   Renting: Renting refers to giving away a copy of software to some other person for temporary use in exchange of a fee.

   Uploading and Downloading: This refers to uploading unauthorized duplicates of licensed and copyrighted software online for general public usage. Any user connected to internet can be a part of such piracy.

5. **What are spams ?**

   Answer : Spamming refers to unwanted or fraud e-mails. These are bulk e-mails that are sent to people generally for advertising, phishing etc. In some cases, spam may consume a lot of memory space.

6. **What are the different types of cyber crimes ?**

   Answer : The different types of cyber crimes are : Hacking, Piracy, Phishing, etc.

7. **What is Netiquette? Give 4 examples.**

   Answer : Etiquette to be followed while using the Internet, is called **Netiquette**. For example :
   (i)   We should not use the computer to harm other people in any way.
   (ii) We should not interfere with other people's work.
   (iii) We should be helpful to people who are learning.
   (iv) We should always use proper language and correct information in our messages.

EXERCISE

Question 1. Fill in the blanks :

   (a) .... is a person's creation which is not in material form.
   (b) .... is the illegal copying of software.
   (c) Etiquette to be followed while using the Internet is called ....
   (d) Spam mails consume a lot of ....
   (e) .... gives the right to the creator that no one can copy the same.

(f) .... is the act of extracting important information from innocent users, by posing as someone reliable.

(g) .... are those people who hack into people's personal information and use them for many wrong intensions.

(h) .... is the process of protecting important and confidential data on the computer system using login Id and password.

Question 2. Choose the correct answer :

(a) It is a distinct name that is used for some kind of goods or services. Its symbol is ®.
   (i) Trade Secrets   (ii) Trademark
   (iii) Copyright   (iv) Patent

(b) These are certain formula or plan that is kept confidential for keeping the uniqueness of an item/property.
   (i) Trade Secrets   (ii) Trademark
   (iii) Copyright   (iv) Patent

(c) It gives the right to the creator that no one can copy the same.
   (i) Trade Secrets   (ii) Trademark
   (iii) Copyright   (iv) Patent

(d) It protects an "idea".
   (i) Trade Secrets   (ii) Trademark
   (iii) Copyright   (iv) Patent

(e) It is an unethical act of breaking into the private zone of any user without the owner's permission.
   (i) Piracy   (ii) Worms
   (iii) Sweeper   (iv) Hacking

Question 3. Identify the following :

(a) It gives the right to the creator that no one can copy the same.

(b) This is a certain formula or plan that is kept confidential for keeping the uniqueness of an item/property.

(c) It protects an "idea".

(d) It causes financial loss to the creative programmers, who make them.

Question 4. Answer in brief :

(a) Why does an "individual's right to privacy" needs protection ?

(b) What is 'data protection on the Internet' ?

(c) What is the difference between a spam and a virus ?

(d) Write four ways of remaining safe online ?

(e) Write two good and two forbidden rules of E-mail Etiquettes.

(f) What is cybercrime ?

(g) What are Intellectual Property Rights ? Explain the various types of Intellectual Property Rights.

(h) What are the protective measures one can use to safegaurd themselves against cyber crimes ?

BEYOND SYLLABUS

Ethical hacking : Hacking is a harmful act. But, it gets converted into a defensive weapon when a company hires a hacker who tries to break into the company's network and identifies if any fragile area is present and might be under threat. That can protect the system from real attacks.

- Ankit Fadia is a famous ethical hacker, born in 1985.
- Just at the age of 15, he authored "An unofficial guide to Ethical Hacking", which became a bestseller.
- He opened up Ethical Hacking as a profession.

Internet Police : Different countries have a police team who monitor the illegal activities over the Internet. The major purposes of the Internet police are to fight cyber crimes, apply censorship and to monitor and manipulate the online public opinion.

APPLICATION PROGRAMS

This chapter consists of programs that apply the various programming tools and logic of conditions and loops. The programs are explained below the program list.

PROGRAM LIST

1. Input the principal, rate and time (annual). Calculate and print the simple interest and compound interest.

   Given that : SI = P.r.t/100 CI = A – P, where A = (P * (1 + r/100) ^ t)

2. Input temperature in Celsius and print the corresponding temperature in Fahrenheit.

   Given that : C/5 = (F-32) / 9

3. Input two variables A, B and interchange their values. Print the values before and after the change.

4. During festive season, a confectioner gives 35% allowance to its employees on their basic pay. Input the basic pay of an employee; calculate the amount of allowance and the total amount payable.

5. Input time in seconds and convert it into total minutes and seconds.

6. In a family summer camp, from each family four members were allowed, that would include two siblings. An offer was such that if the age of the elder sibling was less than 13 years, both of the siblings would get free lunch otherwise both would get a snack packet. Input the age of both siblings in variables A and B. Store the age of the elder sibling in variable G. Print output statements indicating the above offer.

7. In a library, books were given to members for two weeks. Upon late return, they were charged at a rate as per following chart :

Days Late (D)	Late Fine per day (in ₹)
D <= 3	4
D > 3 && D <= 7	8
D > 8 && D <= 15	12
D > 15	20

Input the number of days late. Calculate and print the amount of late fine to be paid.

8. For a password creating team, an extraordinary number was required. The team decided that it would mark a number as extraordinary if it satisfied any one of the following conditions :

   (i)   The number is divisible by 8 and **not** by 6

   (ii) The number is divisible by 12

   Input a number in N, and verify whether it can be used as an extraordinary number or not. In case if it is, then print "The number is extraordinary" and also print from which condition (1st or 2nd) it became valid otherwise print "The number is ordinary."

   Test the following values :

   (i) N = 16   (ii) N = 18   (iii) N = 100   (iv) N = 36
   (v) N = 24

9. A book store was giving a special discount percent to its customers upon the purchase of a certain number of books. The following table shows the detail.

Number of books purchased(N)	Discount (d) on total amount
N >= 100	50%
N <100 && N >= 50	25%
N < 50 and N >= 10	10%
otherwise	4%

   Input the total amount (TA) and the number of books purchased (N). Calculate and print the discount applicable and the amount payable.

10. An amusement park was offering special discount on bulk purchase of tickets, as shown in the following table.

Number of Tickets (T)	Discount Amount (D)
T < 50	5% of Total Ticket Cost
T < 100 & T >= 50	10% of Total Ticket Cost
T < 200 & T >= 100	15% of Total Ticket Cost
T >= 200	25% of Total Ticket Cost

   Input the cost of one ticket (C) and the number of tickets (T). Calculate and print the discount and the amount to pay.

11. Print the given series : 2 5   10 17   26   37 .... up to n terms

12. Print the given series : 2 6   12 20   30   42 56 .... up to n terms

13. Print the given series : 3   6   12 24   48   96 .... up to n terms

14. Print the sum of series : $x + x/3 + x/5 + x/7 + x/9 + ... + x/19$

15. Print the sum of series : $1/2 + 2/3 + 3/4 + 4/5 + ... + 19/20$

16. Print the sum of series : $1 + 2 + 4 + 8 + 16 + 32 + ...$ up to n terms

17. **Prime Number** : It has no factor other than 1 and itself. Input a number and verify whether it is a Prime number or not. For example, 17

18. **Composite Number** : It has a factor other than 1 and itself. Input a number and verify whether it is a Prime number or not. For example, 21

19. **Perfect Number** : It is the sum of its factors, excluding itself or equal to itself. Input a number and verify whether it is a Perfect number or not. For example, $6 = 1 + 2 + 3$

20. **Palindromic Number** : It is a number that reads the same from both directions. Input a number and verify whether it is a Palindromic number or not. For example, 121 , 3553

21. **Amicable Pair of Numbers** : For two numbers P and Q, if the sum of factors of P is Q and sum of factors of Q is P, then P,Q form an amicable pair of numbers. Input two numbers and verify whether they form an amicable pair or not.

22. **Armstrong Number** : It is a number which is equal to the sum of the cubes of its digits. Input a number and verify whether it is an armstrong number or not. For example, 371

23. **Krishnamurthy Number** : It is a number which is equal to the sum of the factorial of its digits. Input a number and verify whether it is a krishnamurthy number or not. For example, 145.

24. **Twin Prime**: For two numbers M and N, if their difference is 2 and both are Prime, then they are called Twin Prime numbers. Input two numbers and verify whether they are Twin prime or not. For example, (17, 19).

25. **Neon Number** : It is a number whose sum of digits of the square of the number is the number itself for example, 9.

26. **Lead Number** : It is a number in which the sum of the even digits is equal to the sum of the odd digits. Input a number and verify whether it is a lead number or not. For example, 1452.

27. **Cyclo Number** : It is a number in which the 1st and the last digit are the same. Input a number and verify whether it is a cyclo number or not. For example, 6216.

28. **Twist Number** : It is a number in which the 1st digit is odd and the last digit is even. Input a number and verify whether it is a twist number or not. For example, 7254.

29. **Micro Number** : It is a number which contains at least one even digit. Input a number and verify whether it is a micro number or not. For example, 5367.

30. **Trunk Number** : It is a number whose reverse is larger than itself. Input a number and verify whether it is a trunk number or not. For example, 4014.

31. **Pearre Partners** : Two numbers M, N are called pearre partners, if the 1st digit of one of them is the last digit of the 2nd and vice versa. Input two numbers and verify whether they are pearre partners or not. For example, (526 , 6735).

32. **Zippo Number** : It is a number in which other than 1st and last digit, all other digits are 0. Input a number and verify whether it is a zippo number or not. For example, 60009.

33. **Histro Pair** : For a number N, its histro pair is made by adding the cube of the odd digits. Input a number and write its histro pair.

    For example, if N = 43558 then its histro pair is $3^3 + 5^3 + 5^3 = 27 + 125 + 125 = 277$.

34. Input a choice(C) and a number(N). If choice is 1, then print the summation of N, (sum of all the integers from 1 to n) , if choice is 2, then print the product of the digits of N. For any other value of choice, print "wrong choice". [Apply switch case statement]

35. Perform addition of two time intervals, where time is given in hh, mm form. Modify the result so that mm ranges from 0 to 59.

SOLUTIONS

1.

Program Idea :
- Input the Principal(p) , rate (r) and time(t).
- Apply the formula of calculation.
- Print the result.

```java
import java.util.*;
class P1
{
    void main()
    {
        double P = 0.0, r = 0.0, t = 0.0 , SI = 0.0 , CI = 0.0, A = 0.0;
        Scanner sc = new Scanner(System.in);
        System.out.println("Enter Principal:"); P = sc.nextDouble();
        System.out.println("Enter rate :"); r = sc.nextDouble();
        System.out.println("Enter time :"); t = sc.nextDouble();
        SI = ( P * r * t)/100;
        System.out.println("Simple Interest = " + SI);
        A = P * Math.pow( ( 1 + r/100), t) ;
        CI = A – P;
        System.out.println("Compound Interest = " + CI);
    }
}
```

OUTPUT

Enter Principal : 1000

Enter rate : 10

Enter time : 5

Simple Interest = 500.0

Compound Interest = 610.514

2.

Program Idea :
- Input the temperature in Celsius (C)

- Modify and apply the formula of calculation.

  $(F-32)/9 = C/5 \rightarrow (F-32) = C/5 * 9 \rightarrow F = (C/5 * 9) + 32$

- Print the result.

```java
import java.util.*;
class P2
{
    void main()
    {
        double C = 0.0, F = 0.0; Scanner sc = new Scanner(System.in);
        System.out.println("Enter temp in Celcius :"); C = sc.nextDouble();
        F = ( C/5 * 9 ) + 32;
        System.out.println(" For C = " + C + " F = " + F);
    }
}
```

OUTPUT

Enter temp in Celcius :100

For C = 100.0 F = 212.0

3.

Program Idea :

- Input the values of two variables A, B.
- Store the value of A in a temporary variable, T.
- Store value of B in A.
- Store value of T in B.
- Print the result.

```java
import java.util.*;
class P3
{
    void main()
    {
        int A=0, B=0, T=0 ;
        Scanner sc = new Scanner(System.in);
        System.out.println("Enter value of A :"); A = sc.nextInt();
        System.out.println("Enter value of B :"); B = sc.nextInt();
        System.out.println(" Given values of A = " + A + " B = " + B);
        T = A;
        A= B;
        B = T;
        System.out.println(" Interchanged values of A = " + A + " B = " + B);
    }
}
```

OUTPUT

Enter value of A :45

Enter value of B :65

 Given values of A = 45 B = 65

 Interchanged values of A = 65 B = 45

4.

Program Idea :

- Input the basic pay bp.
- Calcualte the allowance and total amount payable.
- Print the basic pay, allowance, total amount.

```java
import java.util.*;
class P4
{
    void main()
    {
            double bp = 0.0, alw = 0.0, T = 0.0 ;
            Scanner sc = new Scanner(System.in);
            System.out.println("Enter basic pay :"); bp = sc.nextDouble();
            alw = 35.0/100 * bp;
            T = bp + alw;
            System.out.println(" Basic Pay = " + bp );
            System.out.println(" Allowance = " + alw );
            System.out.println(" Amount payable = " + T );
    }
}
```

OUTPUT

Enter basic pay :5000

Basic Pay = 5000.0

Allowance = 1750.0

Amount payable = 6750.0

5.

Program Idea :

- Input the time in seconds, in integer variable S.[it cannot be a fractional value]
- Number of minutes is the quotient of division by 60 and the remainder in the modified seconds.
- Perform the division and store the values.
- Print the result.

```java
import java.util.*;
class P5
{
```

```java
        void main()
        {
                int TS=0, M=0, S=0 ;
                Scanner sc = new Scanner(System.in);
                System.out.println("Enter total seconds :"); TS = sc.nextInt();
                M = TS/60;
                S = TS%60;
                System.out.println(TS +" Sec  ==  " + M + " Min : " + S + " Sec.");
        }
}
```

OUTPUT

Enter total seconds :100

100 Sec == 1 Min : 40 Sec.

6.

Program Idea :

- Input the age of two siblings A, B.
- Store the larger of A, B in G
- If G <13 , then print Both siblings will get lunch, otherwise print accordingly.

```java
import java.util.*;
class P6
{
    void main()
    {
            int A, B, G ;
            Scanner sc = new Scanner(System.in);
            System.out.println("Enter Age1 : "); A = sc.nextInt();
            System.out.println("Enter Age2 : "); B = sc.nextInt();
            G = (A>B) ?A : B ;
            if(G<13)
            {
                    System.out.println("Both siblings will get lunch.");
            }
            else
            {
                    System.out.println("Both siblings will get snack packet.");
            }
    }
}
```

OUTPUT

Enter Age1 : 11

Enter Age2 : 12

Both siblings will get lunch.

7.

Program Idea :
- Input the number of days late.
- Calculate the fine according to the given conditions
- Print the fine.

```java
import java.util.*;
class P7
{
    void main()
    {
        int DL, Fine ; Scanner sc = new Scanner(System.in);
        System.out.println("Enter the number of days late : "); DL = sc.nextInt();
        if(DL <= 3)
        Fine = 4 * DL;
        elseif(DL > 3 && DL <= 7)
        Fine = 8 *DL;
        elseif(DL>7 && DL <= 15)
        Fine = 12 *DL;
        else
        Fine = 20 * DL;
        System.out.println("Amount of fine " + Fine);
    }
}
```

OUTPUT

Enter the number of days late : 12
Amount of fine : 144

8.

Program Idea :
- Input the number N. Initialize C as 0.
- Verify N using the given conditions and allot C accordingly.
- Verify C for printing the result.

```java
import java.util.*;
class P8
{
    void main()
    {
        int N, C = 0 ; Scanner sc = new Scanner(System.in);
        System.out.println("Enter the number : "); N = sc.nextInt();
        if( N%8 == 0 && N%6!= 0 )
        C = 1;
```

```
            elseif(N%12 == 0 )
            C = 2;
            if( C == 0)
            System.out.println(N + " is an Ordinary Number." );
            else
            System.out.println(N + " is an Extraordinary Number, from condition " +
C);
        }
    }
```

OUTPUT

Enter the number : 16

16 is an Extraordinary Number, from condition 1

Test the following values :

   (i) N = 26   (ii) N = 18   (iii) N = 100   (iv) N = 36   (v) N = 24

9.

Program Idea :

* Input Total amount TA & number of books purchased N.
* Verify N to assign d.
* Calculate the amount payable by applying the discount.
* Print the results.

```java
import java.util.*;
class P9
{
    void main()
    {
        int TA, N; double d, P ; Scanner sc = new Scanner(System.in);
        System.out.println("Enter the Total Amount : "); TA = sc.nextInt();
        System.out.println("Enter the number of books : "); N = sc.nextInt();
        if( N >= 100 )
        d = 50.0/100 * TA ;
        else if( N < 100 && N > = 50 )
        d = 25.0/100 * TA ;
        else if( N < 50 && N > = 10 )
        d = 10.0/100 * TA ;
        else
        d = 4.0/100 * TA ;
        P = TA - d ;
        System.out.println("Number of books purchased : " + N );
        System.out.println("Discount given : " + d );
        System.out.println("Amount payable : " + P );
    }
}
```

Note :
- Data type of TA can be double as well.

OUTPUT

Enter the Total Amount : 2000
Enter the number of books : 54
Number of books purchased : 54
Discount given : 500.0
Amount payable : 1500.0

10.

Program Idea :
- Input cost of one ticket(C), total number of tickets(T).
- Assign discount (D) upon cost of tickets.
- Calculate the amount payable by applying the discount.
- Print the results.

```java
import java.util.*;
class P10
{
    void main()
    {
        int T; double C, d, Tot, Dis, PA ; Scanner sc = new Scanner(System.in);
        System.out.println("Enter the cost of one ticket : "); C = sc.nextDouble();
        System.out.println("Enter the number of tickets : "); T = sc.nextInt();
        if( T < 50 )
        d = 5 ;
        else if( T > = 50 && T < 100 )
        d = 10 ;
        else if( T > = 100 && T < 200 )
        d = 15 ;
        else
        d = 25 ;
        Tot = C*T;
        Dis = d/100 * Tot ;
        PA = Tot - Dis ;
        System.out.println("Total Ticket Cost : " + Tot );
        System.out.println("Discount : " + Dis );
        System.out.println("Amount payable : " + PA );
    }
}
```

OUTPUT

Enter the cost of one ticket : 50
Enter the number of tickets : 50
Total Ticket Cost : 2500.0

Discount : 250.0
Amount payable : 2250.0

11.

Program Idea :

- Identification of the terms of the series : k^{th} term is $(k^2 + 1)$.
- Input n, total number of terms.
- Run a loop of k from 1 to n.
- For each k, calculate term = $k^2 + 1$ and print it.

```java
import java.util.*;
class P11
{
    void main()
    {
        int n, term; Scanner sc = new Scanner(System.in);
        System.out.println("Enter the number of terms : ");
        n = sc.nextInt();
        for(int k = 1 ; k <= n ; k++)
        {
            term = (k*k) + 1;
            System.out.print("   " + term );
        }
    }
}
```

OUTPUT

Enter the number of terms : 9
2 5 10 17 26 37 50 65 82

12.

Program Idea :

- Identification of the terms of the series : k^{th} term is $(k * (k+1))$:
  2nd term = 2 * (2+1) = 2 * 3 = 6
  4th term = 4 * (4+1) = 20
- Input n, total number of terms.
- Run a loop of k from 1 to n.
- For each k, calculate term = k * (k + 1) and print it.

```java
import java.util.*;
class P12
{
    void main()
    {
        int n, term; Scanner sc = new Scanner(System.in);
        System.out.println("Enter the number of terms : ");
        n = sc.nextInt();
```

```
                for(int k = 1 ; k <= n ; k++)
                {
                        term = k * (k + 1);
                        System.out.print("   " + term );
                }
        }
}
```

OUTPUT

Enter the number of terms : 9
2 6 12 20 30 42 56 72 90

13.

Program Idea :

- Identification of the terms of the series : k^{th} term is double of $(k-1)^{th}$ term :

  1st term is given as 3 :

  2nd term = double of 1st term = 2 * 3 = 6.

  3rd term = double of 2nd term = 2 * 6 = 12.

- Input n, total number of terms.
- Assign the first term as term = 3.
- Run a loop of k from 1 to n.
- For each k, print the term and then modify it by its double.

```
import java.util.*;
class P13
{
    void main()
    {
            int n, term = 3 ; Scanner sc = new Scanner(System.in);
            System.out.println("Enter the number of terms : "); n = sc.nextInt();
            for(int k = 1 ; k <= n ; k++)
            {
                    System.out.print("   " + term );
                    term = term * 2 ;
            }
    }
}
```

OUTPUT

Enter the number of terms : 9
3 6 12 24 48 96 192 384 768

14.

Program Idea :

- Identification of the terms of the series :

  terms range is odd numbers in denominator from 1 to 19.

- Input the numerator x, assign sum to 0.
- Run a loop of k from 1 to 19 , with k increasing by 2.
- For each k, calculate term = x / k   and   sum = sum + term.
- Finally out of the loop, print sum.

```java
import java.util.*;
class P14
{
    void main()
    {
        double x, term, sum = 0 ; Scanner sc = new Scanner(System.in);
        System.out.println("Enter the numerator : ");
        x = sc.nextDouble();
        for(int k = 1 ; k <= 19 ; k = k+2)
        {
            term = x / k ;
            sum = sum + term ;
        }
        System.out.println(" Sum = " + sum);
    }
}
```

OUTPUT

Enter the numerator : 2
Sum = 4.266511060319109

15.

Program Idea :
- Identification of the terms of the series :
  terms range in numbers from 1 to 19 (considering the numerators)
- Assign sum to 0.
- Run a loop of k from 1 to 19.
- For each k, calculate term = k / (k+1)   and   sum = sum + term.
- Finally out of the loop, print sum.

```java
import java.util.*;
class P15
{
    void main()
    {
        double x, term, sum = 0; Scanner sc = new Scanner(System.in);
        for(int k = 1 ; k <= 19 ; k++)
        {
            term = (double)k / (k+1);
            sum = sum + term ;
```

```
        }
        System.out.print(" Sum = " + sum);
    }
}
```

OUTPUT

Sum = 16.40226034285632

Note :

- The above program can also be done by using the denominator range from 2 to 20 and making the term accordingly.

16.

Program Idea :

- Identification of the terms of the series : each term is the double of its previous term ranging from 1 to n.
- Assign sum to 0 , term to 1.
- Run a loop of k from 1 to n.
- For each k, calculate sum = sum + term and modify term = 2 * term.
- Finally out of the loop, print sum.

```
import java.util.*;
class P16
{
    void main()
    {
        int n, term=1, sum = 0 ; Scanner sc = new Scanner(System.in);
        System.out.println("Enter the number of terms : ");
        n = sc.nextInt();
        for(int k = 1 ; k < n ; k++)
        {
            sum = sum + term;
            System.out.print( term + " + " );
            term = 2 * term;
        }
        System.out.print( term + " = ");
        sum = sum + term ;
        System.out.print(sum);
    }
}
```

OUTPUT

Enter the number of terms : 8

1 + 2 + 4 + 8 + 16 + 32 + 64 + 128 = 255

17.

Program Idea :

- Input a number N.
- Assume its total factors other than 1 and itself is 0. Assign cf = 0.
- Run a loop of **f** from 2 to N/2.
- For each f, if it is a factor, increment cf by 1.
- Finally out of the loop, if cf – 0, then declare N as prime.

```java
import java.util.*;
class P17
{
    void main()
    {
        Scanner sc = new Scanner(System.in);   int N=0 , cf = 0;
        System.out.println("Enter the number : ");  N = sc.nextInt();
        for(int f = 2 ; f<=N/2 ;f++)      // range of f other than 1 and itself
        {
            if(N%f == 0)     // f is a factor, counter increases
            {
                cf++ ;
            }
        }
        if(cf == 0 )       // no factor other than 1 and itself
        {
            System.out.println( N + " is a Prime Number.");
        }
        else
        {
            System.out.println( N + " is NOT a Prime Number.");
        }
    }
}
```

OUTPUT

Enter the number : 26

26 is NOT a Prime Number.

18.

Program Idea : [Similar to the idea of Prime number] :

- Input a number N.
- Assume it is not composite(C = 0) in the beginning (subject to verification).
- Run a loop of **f** from 2 to N/2 and verify whether N has any factor present in this range, since any factor present in this range will make the number composite, C = 1.

- A single factor found in this range is enough to terminate the loop.
- Finally out of the loop, print N is composite or not.

```java
import java.util.*;
classP18
{
    void main()
    {
        Scanner sc = new Scanner(System.in); int N=0 , C = 0;
        System.out.println("Enter the number : "); N = sc.nextInt();
        for(int f = 2 ; f<=N/2 ;f++)
        {
            if(N%f == 0) // f is a factor other than 1 and itself
            {
                C = 1;
                break ;
            }
        }
        if( C == 1 )
        System.out.println( N + " is a Composite Number.");
        else
        System.out.println( N + " is NOT a Composite Number.");
    }
}
```

OUTPUT

Enter the number :26

26 is a Composite Number.

19.

Program Idea : [Similar to the idea of Prime number] :

- Input a number N, assume sum = 0.
- Run a loop of **f** from 1 to N/2 and for each factor present in this range add it to sum.
- Finally out of the loop, verify whether sum = N, if so, then N is a Perfect Number.

```java
import java.util.*;
class P19
{
    void main()
    {
        Scanner sc = new Scanner(System.in); int N=0 , cf = 0 , sum = 0;
        System.out.println("Enter the number : "); N = sc.nextInt();
        for(int f = 1 ; f<=N/2 ;f++)
        {
```

```java
                if(N%f == 0)
                {
                        sum = sum + f;
                }
            }
            if( sum == N )
            {
                    System.out.println( N + " is a Perfect Number.");
            }
            else
            {
                    System.out.println( N + " is NOT a Perfect Number.");
            }
        }
    }
```

OUTPUT

Enter the number : 28

28 is a Perfect Number.

20.

Program Idea :

- Input a number N.
- Create its reverse(R) by extracting its digits.
- Finally out of the loop, verify whether N = R, if so, then N is a Palindromic Number.

```java
import java.util.*;
class P20
{
    void main()
    {
            Scanner sc = new Scanner(System.in); int N=0 , d , R = 0;
            System.out.println("Enter the number : "); N = sc.nextInt(); int cN = N;
            while ( cN> 0 )
            {
                    d = cN % 10;
                    R = R * 10 + d ;
                    cN = cN / 10;
            }
            if( R == N )
            {
                    System.out.println( N + " is a Palindromic Number.");
            }
```

```java
            else
            {
                    System.out.println( N + " is NOT a Palindromic Number.");
            }
        }
}
```

OUTPUT

Enter the number : 1551

1551 is a Palindromic Number.

21.

Program Idea :

- Input two numbers N1 & N2.
- Find the sum of factors N1 in sum1 and sum of factors N2 in sum2.
- Then check sum1 = = sum2.
- Print the results.

```java
import java.util.*;
class P21
{
    void main()
    {
        Scanner sc = new Scanner ( System.in );
        int N1 = 0 , N2 = 0 , sum1 = 0 , sum2 = 0 ;
        System.out.println( "Enter two numbers number : " );
        N1 = sc.nextInt(); N2 = sc.nextInt();
        System.out.print("\nFactors of " + N1 + " : ");
        for ( int f = 1 ; f<=N1/2 ; f++)
        {
            if( N1 % f == 0)
            {
                    System.out.print("  " + f);
                    sum1 = sum1 + f ;
            }
        }
        System.out.print("\nFactors of " + N2 + " : ");
        for ( int f = 1 ; f<=N2/2 ; f++)
        {
            if( N2 % f == 0)
            {
                    System.out.print("  " + f);
                    sum2 = sum2 + f;
            }
```

```
            }
        if( sum1 == N2 &&  sum2 == N1 )
        System.out.print("\n"+ N1 + "  & " + N2 + " make an Amicable Pair." );
        else
        System.out.print("\n"+ N1 + "  & " + N2 + " do NOT make an Amicable
                                                        Pair.");

        }
    }
```

OUTPUT

Enter two numbers number :

284

220

Note :

- Also verify 1184, 1210

Factors of 284 : 1   2   4   71   142
Factors of 220 : 1   2   4   5   10   11   20   22   44   55   110
284 & 220 make an Amicable Pair.

22.

Program Idea :

- Input a number N.
- Add the cube of the digits in sum.
- Finally out of the loop, verify whether sum = N, if so, then N is an Armstrong Number.

```
import java.util.*;
class P22
{
    void main()
    {
        Scanner sc = new Scanner(System.in); int N=0 , d , sum = 0;
        System.out.println("Enter the number : "); N = sc.nextInt(); int cN = N ;
        while ( cN> 0 )
        {
            d = cN % 10;
            sum =sum + d*d*d;
            cN = cN / 10;
        }
        if( sum == N )
        {
            System.out.println( N + " is an Armstrong Number.");
        }
        else
        {
```

198

```java
            System.out.print( N + " is NOT an Arnstrong Number.");
        }
    }
}
```

OUTPUT

Enter the number : 371

371 is an Armstrong Number.

23.

Program Idea :

- Input a number N.
- Extract the digits.
- For each digit, find its factorial and add it to sum.
- Refresh the variable storing factorial of each digit.
- Finally, verify whether sum = N, if so, then N is a Krishnamurthy Number.

```java
import java.util.*;
class P23
{
    void main()
    {
        Scanner sc = new Scanner(System.in); int N=0 , d , sum = 0;
        System.out.println("Enter the number : "); N = sc.nextInt();
        int cN = N , p = 1;   // cN is the copy of N
        while ( cN> 0 )
        {
            d = cN % 10; //extracting digits
            for(int k = 1; k<=d; k++)
            {
                    p = p * k;
            }
            sum =sum + p;
            p = 1; // refreshing p for next round
            cN = cN / 10; // modifying cN for next round
        }
        if( sum == N )
        {
            System.out.println( N + " is a Krishnamurthy Number.");
        }
        else
        {
            System.out.print( N + " is NOT a Krishnamurthy Number.");
```

```
                }
        }
}
```

OUTPUT

Enter the number : 145

145 is a Krishnamurty Number.

24.

Program Idea :

- Input two numbers, M, N.
- Verify whether both M, N are Prime or not. [Assuming them to be prime in the beginning, and then if any factor is found, it loses its prime status]
- Find their difference in d.
- Finally, verify whether d == 2 and both numbers are prime, if so, then M & N are twin pair.

```java
import java.util.*;
class P24
{
    void main()
    {
        Scanner sc = new Scanner(System.in); int M = 0 , N = 0, pM = 0 , pN = 0;
        System.out.println("Enter first number : "); M = sc.nextInt();
        System.out.println("Enter second number : "); N = sc.nextInt();
        for(int f = 2 ; f<=M/2; f++)
        {
            if(M % f == 0)
            {
                pM = 1;
                break;
            }
        }
        for(int f = 2 ; f<=N/2; f++)
        {
            if(N% f == 0)
            {
                pN = 1;
                break;
            }
        }
        int d = M-N;
```

```
        if ( d<0)
        d = d*(-1);
        if(pM == 0 &&pN == 0 &&d == 2)
        System.out.println( "( " + M + " , " + N + ") is a Twin Prime Pair .");
        else
        System.out.println( "( " + M + " , " + N + ") is NOT a Twin Prime
                                                        Pair .");

    }

}
```

OUTPUT

Enter first number : 29
Enter second number : 31
(29, 31) is a Twin Prime Pair .

25.

Program Idea :
- Input a number, N.
- Find its square and the sum of its digits in sum.
- Finally, verify whether sum = N, if so then N is a Neon Number.

```
import java.util.*;
class P25
{
    void main()
    {
            Scanner sc = new Scanner(System.in); int N=0, d, sum = 0;
            System.out.println("Enter the number : "); N = sc.nextInt();
            int SQN = N*N; int cs = SQN;
            while ( cs> 0 )           // to add the digits of square of N
            {
                d = cs % 10;
                sum = sum + d ;
                cs = cs / 10;
            }
            if( sum == N )
            System.out.println( N + " is a NEON Number.");
            else
            System.out.print( N + " is NOT a NEON Number.");
    }
}
```

OUTPUT

Enter the number : 9
9 is a NEON Number.

26.

Program Idea :

- Input a number, N.
- Extract its digits.
- For each digit, if it is even, add it to **se** and if it is odd, add it to **sd**.
- Finally, verify whether se = sd, if so then N is a Lead Number.

```java
import java.util.*;
class P26
{
    void main()
    {
        Scanner sc = new Scanner(System.in); int N=0 ,se = 0, sd = 0 ;
        System.out.println("Enter the number : "); N = sc.nextInt();
        int cN = N, digit = 0;
        while(cN> 0)
        {
            digit = cN%10;
            if( digit %2 == 0)
            {
                se = se + digit ;
            }
            else
            {
                sd = sd + digit ;
            }
            cN = cN/10;
        }
        if( se == sd )
        {
            System.out.println( N + " is a LEAD Number.");
        }
        else
        {
            System.out.print( N + " is NOT a LEAD Number.");
        }
    }
}
```

OUTPUT

Enter the number : 1452

1452 is a LEAD Number.

27.

Program Idea :

- Input a number, N.
- Store the last digit in LDigit.
- To extract the first digit, go on dividing the number by 10 as long as the number is more than or equal to 10.
- Finally, verify whether FDigit= LDigit, if so, then N is a Cyclo Number.

```java
import java.util.*;
class P27
{
    void main()
    {
        Scanner sc = new Scanner(System.in); int N=0;
        System.out.println("Enter the number : "); N = sc.nextInt();
        int cN = N, FDigit = 0, LDigit=0;
        LDigit = cN%10;
        while(cN>=10)
        {
            cN = cN/10;
        }
        FDigit = cN;
        if(FDigit == LDigit )
        System.out.println( N + " is a Cyclo Number.");
        else
        System.out.print( N + " is NOT a Cyclo Number.");
    }
}
```

OUTPUT

Enter the number : 845238

845238 is a Cyclo Number.

28.

Program Idea : [similar to previous program idea] :

- Input a number, N.
- Store the last digit in LDigit.
- To extract the first digit, go on dividing the number by 10 as long as the number is more than or equal to 10.
- Finally, verify whether FDigit is odd and LDigit is even, if both are then N is a Twist Number.

```java
import java.util.*;
class P28
```

```java
{
    void main()
    {
        Scanner sc = new Scanner(System.in);
        int N=0;
        System.out.println("Enter the number : "); N = sc.nextInt();
        int cN = N, FDigit = 0, LDigit=0;
        LDigit = cN%10;
        while(cN>=10)
        {
            cN = cN/10;
        }
        FDigit = cN;
        if( FDigit%2 != 0   &&   LDigit%2 == 0 )
        {
            System.out.println( N + " is a Twist Number.");
        }
        else
        {
            System.out.print( N + " is NOT a Twist Number.");
        }
    }
}
```

OUTPUT

Enter the number : 7254
7254 is a Twist Number.

29.

Program Idea : [similar to program idea of Composite number] :

* Input a number, N.
* Assume it is not Micro, mc = 0.
* Extract the digits and for each digit, verify whether it is even or not.
* If any even digit is found, set mc to 1 and terminate the search.
* Finally if mc = 1, then N is a Micro number.

```java
import java.util.*;
class P29
{
    void main()
    {
        Scanner sc = new Scanner(System.in);
        int N=0;
        System.out.println("Enter the number : "); N = sc.nextInt();
```

```java
        int cN = N, mc=0 , d=0;
        while(cN>0)
        {
                d = cN%10;
                if(d %2 == 0)
                {
                        mc = 1;
                        break;
                }
                cN = cN/10;
        }
        if( mc == 1 )
        System.out.println( N + " is a Micro Number as digit " + d + " is even.");
        else
        System.out.print( N + " is NOT a Micro Number.");
    }
}
```

OUTPUT

Enter the number : 5367

5367 is a Micro Number as digit 6 is even.

30.

Program Idea : [similar to program idea of Palindromic number] :

- Input a number, N.
- Calculate its reverse in R.
- If the reverse is larger than N then N is a Trunk number.

```java
import java.util.*;
class P30
{
    void main()
    {
        Scanner sc = new Scanner(System.in);
        int N=0 , d , R = 0;
        System.out.println("Enter the number : ");
        N = sc.nextInt();
        int cN = N ;
        while ( cN> 0 )
        {
                d = cN % 10;
                R = R * 10 + d ;
                cN = cN / 10;
```

```
                }
                if( R > N )
                {
                        System.out.println( N + " is a Trunk Number.");
                }
                else
                {
                        System.out.println( N + " is NOT a Trunk Number.");
                }
        }
}
```

OUTPUT

Enter the number : 4104

4104 is NOT a Trunk Number.

31.

Program Idea : [similar to the program idea of Cyclo number] :
- Input two numbers, M, N.
- Store the first and last digit of M in MFDigit and MLDigit.
- Store the first and last digit of N in NFDigit and NLDigit.
- Verify whether MFDigit = NLDigit and MLDigit = NFDigit.
- If both the conditions are true then M, N form Pearre Partners.

```
import java.util.*;
class P31
{
    void main()
    {
            Scanner sc = new Scanner(System.in);
            int M=0 , N=0 ;
            System.out.println("Enter M : ");
            M = sc.nextInt();
            System.out.println("Enter N : ");
            N = sc.nextInt();
            int cM = M, MFDigit = 0, MLDigit = cM%10;
            while(cM>=10)
            {
                    cM = cM/10;
            }
            MFDigit = cM;
            int cN = N, NFDigit = 0, NLDigit = cN%10;
```

```
        while(cN>=10)
        {
                cN = cN/10;
        }
        NFDigit = cN;
        if(MFDigit == NLDigit && MLDigit == NFDigit)
        System.out.println( M + "  and  " + N + " are Pearre Partners.");
        else
        System.out.println(  M + "  and  " + N + " are NOT Pearre Partners");
    }
}
```

OUTPUT

Enter M : 62

Enter N : 25146

62 and 25146 are Pearre Partners.

32.

Program Idea :

- Input a number in N, assume it is valid Zippo Number, valid = 1
- Verify digit, if number <100 then valid = 0
- Verify the last digit, if 0 then valid = 0
- verify the digits other than the last and the first digit, if any digit is non zero here, then valid = 0

PROGRAM

```java
import java.util.*;
class P32
{
    void main()
    {
        Scanner sc = new Scanner(System.in); int N=0 , valid = 1;
        System.out.println("Enter N : "); N = sc.nextInt(); int cN = N;
        if(cN<100)
        {
                valid = 0;
        }
        if( cN%10 == 0)
        {
                valid = 0;
        }
        cN = cN/10;
        while(cN>10)
        {
```

```
                        int d = cN%10;
                        if( d != 0)
                        {
                                valid =0;
                                break;
                        }
                        cN=cN/10;
                }
                if( valid == 1)
                System.out.println( N + " is a Zippo number.");
                else
                System.out.print( N + " is NOT a Zippo number.");
        }
}
```

OUTPUT

Enter N : 101

101 is a Zippo number.

33.

Program Idea :

- Input a number in N , assume s = 0.
- Extract its digits in d.
- For each d, if it is odd, add its cube to s.
- Finally, print s.

```
import java.util.*;
class P33
{
    void main()
    {
        Scanner sc = new Scanner(System.in); int N=0 , s = 0, d;
        System.out.println("Enter N : "); N = sc.nextInt(); int cN = N;
        while(cN>0)
        {
            d = cN%10;
            if( d%2 != 0)
            {
                s = s + d*d*d;
            }
            cN=cN/10;
        }
        System.out.println( "Histro pair of " + N + " is " + s);
    }
}
```

OUTPUT

Enter N : 43558

Histro pair of 43558 is 277

34.

Program Idea :

- Input the number in N , choice in C.
- Apply switch case to choose C and perform accordingly.

```java
import java.util.*;
class P34
{
    void main()
    {
        int N, C ;  Scanner sc = new Scanner (System.in);
        System.out.print("\n Enter the Choice : ");
        C = sc.nextInt();
        System.out.print("\n Enter the number : ");
        N = sc.nextInt();
        switch (C)
        {
            case 1 :  int s = 0;
                      for(int k=1; k<=N; k++)
                      {
                         s = s + k;
                      }
                      System.out.print("\n Summation of " + N + " = " + s );
                      break;
            case 2 :  int p = 1; int cN = N;
                      while (cN> 0 )
                      {
                         int d = cN%10;
                         p = p * d;
                         cN /= 10;
                      }
                      System.out.print("\n Product of digits of " + N + " = " + p );
                      break;
            default :System.out.print(" Wrong Choice" );
        }
    }
}
```

OUTPUT

Enter the Choice : 2

Enter the number : 452

Product of digits of 452 = 40

35.

Program Idea :

- Input the two time intervals.
- Add the hours, and add the mins.
- If total min>=60, then increase total hours by 1 and decrease total min by 60.
- Print the result.

```java
import java.util.*;
class P35
{
    void main()
    {
        int hh1, mm1, hh2, mm2, hh3, mm3; Scanner sc = new Scanner (System.in);
        System.out.print("\n Enter the 1st Time hh : "); hh1 = sc.nextInt();
        System.out.print("\n Enter the 1st Time mm : "); mm1 = sc.nextInt();

        System.out.print("\n Enter the 2nd Time hh : "); hh2 = sc.nextInt();
        System.out.print("\n Enter the 2nd Time mm : "); mm2 = sc.nextInt();

        hh3 = hh1 + hh2;
        mm3 = mm1 + mm2;

        if(mm3 >= 60)
        {
            hh3 = hh3 + 1 ;
            mm3 = mm3 - 60;
        }
        System.out.print("\n Total Time is " + hh3 + " : " + mm3 );
    }
}
```

OUTPUT

Enter the 1st Time hh : 5

Enter the 1st Time mm : 45

Enter the 2nd Time hh : 1

Enter the 2nd Time mm : 45

Total Time is 7 : 30

Chapter

ANSWER SHEET
(Answers of Selected Questions)

CHAPTER 1 : ELEMENTARY CONCEPT OF OBJECT AND CLASS

Answer 1 :

(a) A **class** is a blueprint to create objects. In other words, we can say that a class provides a definition for an item.

An **object** is an instance of a class. The object brings a class to the real world.

(b) It is a kind of programming language in which classes generate objects and define their structure, like a blue print and the objects are created to implement the tasks as intended by the computer program by interacting among each other : Java, C++ are some examples of OOP Languages.

(c) Main features of OOP language are :

(i) Encapsulation : All data and methods are enclosed in a class.

(ii) Inheritance : A derived (child) class being able to access data/methods of its base (parent) class. This feature helps in code reusability.

(iii) Polymorphism : Ability of methods to have same name but to behave differently under different situations.

(iv) Abstraction : Ability to apply the method without knowing the method details.

(d) Abstraction shows only the important things while hiding the background functionality.

Encapsulation, on the other hand, is a concept in which all data and methods are enclosed in a class.

(e) Message passing is done using methods or functions. Message passing is also known as inter-process communication.

Answer 2 : Objects of class

(a) car

(b) students

(c) pens

(d) 100 rupee notes

(e) books

(f) audience, movie

(g) guests, flower bouquet
(h) passengers
(i) computers
(j) wrist watches

Answer 3 :

(a) Encapsulation   (b) Abstraction   (c) Polymorphism
(d) Inheritance   (e) Abstraction

CHAPTER 2 : INTRODUCTION TO JAVA-DATA VALUES AND TYPES

Answer 1 :

(a) ;
(b) =
(c) single
(d) token
(e) controlling

Answer 2 :

(a) Explicit & Implicit Conversion

Implicit	Explicit
In this kind of type conversion, the resulting data types are not specified and are chosen by the complier. The compiler prefers not to lose any part of data value.	In this kind of type conversion, the resulting data types are explicitly specified by the programmer.

(b) Keywords & Identifiers

Keywords	Identifiers
Keywords are words that have a specific meaning.	Identifiers are names given to variables, constants, classes and methods. Keywords can't be used as identifiers.

(c) Primitive & Non Primitive data types.

Primitive	Non-Primitive
Primitive data types are readily available for programmer's use. Java has eight primitive data types	Non primitive data types are generally made up of multiple primitive data types.
Eg : int, char, boolean, long, float, double	Eg : Classes and arrays.

(d) Short & int

Short	Int
Size 2 bytes	Size 4 bytes
Range is from-32,768 to + 32,767	Range is from -2^{31} to $+ 2^{31}-1$

(e) Boolean & Character Literal

Character Literal	Boolean
It contains Keyboard Characters	It contains values of type True or False.
Size is of 16 bits.	Size is of 1 byte.

Answer 3 :

(a) True

(b) False

(c) False

(d) False

(e) True

Answer 4 :

(a) It is the smallest identifiable part of a program. Following are tokens in Java- Keywords, Identifiers, Literals, Separators and Operators.

(b) These are constants that have a fixed value of any of the data-types. They can be any number, text, or other information that represents a value.

(c) It is the smallest unit of a program that gets executed. Statements in Java are terminated by a semicolon (;).

(d) Identifiers have to follow certain rules :

    (i)   The first character of an identifier must be a letter, or an underscore (_), or a dollar sign($).

    (ii) The rest of the characters in the identifier can be a letter, underscore, dollar sign, or digit. Note that spaces are NOT allowed in identifiers.

    (iii) Identifiers are case-sensitive. This means that age and Age are different identifiers.

    (iv) Java's Keywords/reserved words cannot be used as identifiers.

CHAPTER 3 : OPERATORS IN JAVA

Answer 1.

(a) An operator is a symbol that indicates the operation of a task involving operands. There are different forms and types of operators that return some result upon completion of their operation.

(b) Unary operator takes only one value for its operation. For example, unary + , unary - , increment (++) and decrement(- -) .

    A binary operator takes two operands and calculates a result to return. For example, the arithmetic operators commonly used for calculations such as   +   -   *   /   %

    a + 6, p * q

    A ternary operator takes three operands and returns accordingly. Java uses ternary operator for small conditional values.

    int d = (a > b) ? a : b;

(c) There are many types of operators :

    (a) Simple Assignment Operator

    (b) Arithmetic Operator

    (c) Relational Operator

    (d) Logical Operator

    (e) Increment or decrement operator

    (f) Short hand operator

(d) These are a combination of arithmetic operator and assignment operator. They are of the form N op= V where N is a variable, V is value of modification, op is Java binary operator and op = is called shorthand operator.

(e) When more than one operator is present in an expression, the operator having higher precedence / priority get operated first.

Answer 2.

(a)

System.out.println()	System.out.print()
This statement prints the argument inside the bracket and then the cursor waits in the next line.	This statement prints the argument inside the bracket and then the cursor waits at the end of the printed sentence.

(b)

Increment Operator	Decrement Operator
It increases the value by 1	It decreases the value by 1.
If applied as prefix then at first the variable's value increases and then the value is used.	If applied as prefix then at first the variable's value decreases and then the value is used.
If applied as postfix then at first the variable's value is used and then the value is incremented.	If applied as postfix then at first the variable's value is used and then the value is decremented.

(c)

Assignment Operator	Relational Operator
The '=' is the so-called assignment operator and is used to assign the result of the expression on the right side of the operator to the variable on the left side.	The '==' is the so-called equality comparison operator and is used to check whether the two expressions on both sides are equal or not. It returns true if they are equal, and false if they are not.

(d)

Counter	Accumulator
A counter is a variable that is used for counting. It increases by a fixed value.	An accumulator is a variable that is used for accumulating or storing a result formed by accumulation. It gets modified by some unknown value.

(e)

New Operator	Dot Operator
Keyword new is used to allocate memory to an object at runtime. Such memory allocation is called dynamic memory allocation.	. (dot) operator is used to access elements/members of an object through its class name or reference variable.

Answer 3 :

(a)   FALSE

(b)   TRUE

(c)   FALSE

(d)   TRUE

(e)   TRUE

Answer 4 :

(a)   ! (NOT)

(b)   prefix

(c)   = operator

(d)   Logical operator

(e)   accumulator

CHAPTER 4 : INPUT IN JAVA

Answer 1.

(a)   import

(b)   A package contains built-in methods that can be used in a program.

Answer 2.

(a)   Scanner - java.util   (b)   Math – java.lang   (c)   Calendar –java.util

(d)   BufferedReader – java.io   (e)   StringTokenizer – java.util

Answer 3.

(a)   Syntax Error : During compilation, a Syntax Error is reported by the compiler if the program is not written as per specification. They are easier to detect with the help of the compiler. For example r = a x b; Reason x is not an operator.

Logical Error : This kind of error occurs when the logic of the program is not correct. For example + symbol is used for multiplication. The compiler cannot detect logical error and so need more care to be detected.

(b)   Math.pow(p, q) : to calculate the value of p to the power of q (p^q).

Math.sqrt(p) : to calculate the value of square root of argument p.

Answer 4 :

(a)   DF = 23.0   DC = 24.0

(b)   Ans : 4.64

(c)   DE = 63.0

(d)   A = 48

(e)   R = 28

Answer 5.

1.
```
class Q1
{
    void main()
    {
        int totalGrass=230;
        int eachCow=15;
        double numberOfCows=(totalGrass/eachCow);
        numberOfCows=Math.floor(numberOfCows);
        System.out.println("Number of Cows he can feed are:"+numberOfCows);
    }
}
```

2. numberOfFriends =(totalMoney/eachBag);
    numberOfFriends = Math.floor(numberOfFriends);

3. Math.sqrt(12.25);

4. Math.pow(3.375,3);

5. int dif=A-B;
    Math.abs(dif);

6. Math.ceil(22.45)
    Math.ceil(27.55)

7. Math.ceil(138.65)

8. Math.round(25.87)
    Math.round(89.25)
    Math.round(117.98)

9. Math.pow(5,4)

10. T=757

CHAPTER 5 : CONDITIONAL CONSTRUCTS IN JAVA

Answer 1 :

(a) Three types of loops are : for loop, while loop, do... while loop

(b) These operators help in creating a condition.

Java has six relational operators, shown in the following table :

Operator	Use	Operator	Use
>	Greater than	<=	Less than or equal to
<	Less than	==	Comparison of Equality
>=	Greater Than or Equal to	!=	Comparison of Inequality

(c) Logical Operators : These operators help to connect more than one condition. Java has three logical operators :

Operator	Use	Result
!	NOT	Reverses the result of a given condition
&&	AND	Result is True only if all the conditions are True
||	OR	Result is True if any one of the conditions is True

A condition may be a single or composite. A composite condition is made up of multiple conditions which are connected by using Logical Operators (AND and OR).

(d) In switch case construct, if break is not given then, all the statements that appear below the matching case, get executed. This situation is called Fall Through.

(e) In Switch Case statement, default becomes active when none of the cases match. Default and the block present under it should appear at last.

Default in switch...case is optional. Without its presence, there will be no action in the switch...case block, when none of the cases will match.

It is equivalent to the final else statement of if...else.

Answer 2 :   (a) R = 400   (b) R = 200   (c) R = 100   (d) R = 22

Answer 3 :   (a) Liechtenstein   (b) France   (c) Vilnius   (d) San Marino17

Answer 4 :

```
(a)  if ( p == 9 )                        (b)  if ( q != 9 )
     {                                          {
         System.out.print ( " Nine );               System.out.print   ("   Not"
     }                                                                    Nine ");
                                                }

(c)  if ( w >= 9 )                        (d)  if ( t != 9 )
     {                                          {
         System.out.print ( " Beyond Nine" );       System.out.print ( "No" );
     }                                          }

(e)  switch  (k)                          (f)  switch  (m)
     {                                          {
     case 23 : System.out.print("Red");         case 9 : System.out.print(99);
               break ;                                    break;
     default : System.out.print("Blue");        default : system.out.print(22);
     }                                          }
```

(g) if (w > 9)
```
    {
        System.out.print ( "Above Nine" );
    }
    else
    {
        System.out.print ( " Below Nine" );
    }
```

(h) d = (p > q) ? p : q;

(i)   g = (h != 0) ? 10 : 20;

(j)   r = (p == 5) ? 8 : 4;

Answer 5 :

(a)

```
import java.util.* ;
class Roshni
{
    void main ( )
    {
        Scanner sc=  new Scanner ( System.in );
        double bookcost1 = 0.0, bookcost2 = 0 , dis1 = 0, dis2 = 0, total = 0;
        System.out.println( " Enter the cost of book1 :  " );
        bookcost1 = sc.nextDouble();
        System.out.println( " Enter the cost of book2 :  " );
        bookcost2 = sc.nextDouble();
        if (bookcost1 > 1000)
        {
            dis1 = 0.35 * bookcost1;
        }
        else
        {
            dis1 = 0.10 * bookcost1;
        }
        if (bookcost2 > 1000)
        {
            dis2 = 0.35 * bookcost2;
        }
        else
        {
            dis2 = 0.10 * bookcost2;
        }
        total = (bookcost1 - dis1) + ( bookcost2 - dis2 );
        System.out.println( " Discount on book1 :  " + dis1);
        System.out.println( " Discount on book2 :  " + dis2);
        System.out.println( " Total amount payable :  " + total );
    }
}
```

Output :

Enter the cost of book1 : 2000

Enter the cost of book2 : 575

Discount on book1 : 700.0

Discount on book2 : 57.5

Total amount payable : 1817.5

(b)

```java
import java.util.* ;
class ProfitLoss
{
    void main()
    {
        Scanner sc=  new Scanner ( System.in );
        double spcamera , cpguitar, cptabla, cptotal;
        System.out.println( " Enter the sel price of SLR Camera :  " );
        spcamera = sc.nextDouble();
        System.out.println( " Enter the cost price of Guitar :  " );
        cpguitar = sc.nextDouble();
        System.out.println( " Enter the cost price of Tabla :  " );
        cptabla = sc.nextDouble();
        cptotal = cpguitar + cptabla;
        if (spcamera>cptotal )
        {
            double pr = spcamera - cptotal;
            double prpt = pr/cptotal * 100;
            System.out.println(" Profit incurred  " + pr + " Profit Percent = " +
                                                                    prpt );
        }
        elseif (spcamera<cptotal )
        {
            double loss= spcamera - cptotal;
            double losspt = loss/cptotal * 100;
            System.out.println(" Loss incurred  " + loss + " Loss Percent = " +
                                                                    losspt );
        }
        else
        {
            System.out.println( " Neither Profit nor Loss ");
        }
    }
}
```

```java
//Output
Enter the sel price of SLR Camera :  35000
Enter the cost price of Guitar :  6000
Enter the cost price of Tabla :  8000
Profit incurred  21000.0 Profit Percent = 150.0
```

(c)

```java
import java.util.* ;
class Drama
{
    void main()
    {
        Scanner sc=  new Scanner ( System.in ); int daynum;
        System.out.println( " Enter the day number :  " ); daynum = sc.nextInt();
        switch(daynum)
        {
            case 1 :    System.out.print( " Sunday " );
                        break;
            case 2 :    System.out.print( " Monday. Special Coach Day. " );
                        break;
            case 3 :    System.out.print( " Tuesday " );
                        break;
            case 4 :    System.out.print( " Wednesday " );
                        break;
            case 5 :    System.out.print( " Thursday. Special Coach Day. " );
                        break;
            case 6 :    System.out.print( " Friday " );
                        break;
            case 7 :    System.out.print( " Saturday " );
                        break;
            default :   System.out.print( " Wrong Input " );
        }
    }
}
//Output
Enter the day number :  2
Monday. Special Coach Day.
```

(d)

```java
import java.util.*;
class Factor
{
```

```java
        void main()
        {
                Scanner sc= new Scanner ( System.in ); int M, L;
                System.out.println( " Enter the value of M :  " );  M = sc.nextInt();
                System.out.println( " Enter the value of L :  " );  L = sc.nextInt();
                if( L%M == 0)
                {
                    if( L %2 == 0)
                    {
                            System.out.print (M + " is an Even Factor of " + L );
                    }
                    else
                    {
                            System.out.print (M + " is an Odd Factor of " + L );
                    }
                    else
                    {
                            System.out.print (M + " is not a Factor of " + L );
                    }
                }
        }
//Output
 Enter the value of M :  450
 Enter the value of L :  900
450 is an Even Factor of 900
(e)
    import java.util.*;
    class Stavensev
    {
        void main()
        {
                Scanner sc= new Scanner ( System.in );
                int S ;
                System.out.println( " Enter the value of S :  " );  S = sc.nextInt();
                if( S > 700 && S%77 == 0)
                {
                        System.out.print (S + " is a Stravensev Number" );
                }
                else if( S < 77  && 700%S == 0)
                {
                        System.out.print (S + " is a Stravensev Number" );
```

```java
                }
                else
                {
                        System.out.print( S + " is NOT a Stravensev Number" );
                }
        }
    }
//Output
Enter the value of S :  847
847 is a Stravensev Number
```

(f)

```java
    import java.util.* ;
    class Temperature
    {
        void main()
        {
                Scanner sc=  new Scanner ( System.in ); double t1, t2 ; int unit;
                System.out.println( " Enter the value of Temperature :   " );
                t1 = sc.nextDouble();
                System.out.println( " Enter the unit of Temp ( 1 for Celcius, 2 for Kelvin
                                                                    :  " );
                unit = sc.nextInt();
                if( unit == 1)
                {
                    t2 = t1 - 273;
                    System.out.println ("Temp in Celcius : " + t1 );
                    System.out.println("Equivalent Temp in Kelvin : " + t2 );
                }
                else if( unit == 2)
                {
                    t2 = t1 + 273;
                    System.out.println ("Temp in Kelvin : " + t1 );
                    System.out.println("Equivalent Temp in Celcius : " + t2 );
                }
                else
                {
                    System.out.print( "Sorry , no such Unit" );
                }
        }
    }
/* Output
Enter the value of Temperature :  273
Enter the unit of Temperature( 1 for Celcius, 2 for Kelvin :  1
```

Temp in Celcius : 273.0
Equivalent Temp in Kelvin : 0.0

Enter the value of Temperature : 100
Enter the unit of Temperature(1 for Celcius, 2 for Kelvin : 2
Temp in Kelvin : 100.0
Equivalent Temp in Celcius : 373.0
*/
(g)

```java
import java.util.*;
class Magazine
{
    void main()
    {
        Scanner sc=  new Scanner ( System.in );
        double p= 0 , dis1= 0 , dis2 = 0, amt ; int fp = 0;
        System.out.println( " Enter the price of the advertisement :  " );
        p = sc.nextDouble();
        System.out.println( " Full page ( 1 for Yes ) :  " );  fp = sc.nextInt();
        dis1 = p * 5.0/100;
        amt = p - dis1;
        if(fp == 1)
        {
            dis2 = amt * 4.0/100;
            amt = amt - dis2;
        }
        System.out.println( " Discount = " + (dis1 + dis2) + " and Amount
                                        to pay =  " + amt );
    }
}
/* Output
Enter the price of the advertisement :  1000
Full page ( 1 for Yes ) :  2
Discount = 50.0 and Amount to pay =  950.0

Enter the price of the advertisement :  1000
Full page ( 1 for Yes ) :  1
Discount = 88.0 and Amount to pay =  912.0
*/
```

(h)

```java
import java.util.*;
class Emotion
{
    void main()
```

```java
        {
                Scanner sc=  new Scanner ( System.in );
                int A = 0, H= 0 ; double E = 0;
                System.out.println( " Enter the age :  " ) ;  A = sc.nextInt();
                System.out.println( " Enter the height :  " ) ;  H = sc.nextInt();
                if( A <= 12 )
                {
                    E = 5  + ( 0.45 * A + 0.5 * H ) / ( A + H );
                }
                else
                {
                    E = 15 + ( 0.26 * A + 0.35 * H ) / ( 2*A - H);
                }

                System.out.println( " Emotion = " + E );
        }
    }
/* Output
Enter the age :  10
Enter the height : 129
Emotion = 5.496402877697841
*/
```

CHAPTER 6 : ITERATIVE CONSTRUCTS IN JAVA

Answer 1 :

(a) Loops are used to perform repetitive tasks.

(b) Jump statements are used to take the control to another location in the code. The two jump statements in Java are break and continue.

(c) A loop that repeats infinite times is called an infinite loop.

(d) For Loop : When the number of iterations and the amount of change in the loop counter is known, this loop is preferred. It is an entry – controlled loop.

While Loop : When the change in loop counter is not known and the number of iterations is also not fixed, then while loop is used. It is an entry – controlled loop.

(e) In case of an exit controlled loop, the condition is tested after executing the block of code. The block of code under exit controlled loop gets executed at least once, even if the loop condition is false.

In case of an entry controlled loop, the condition is tested before executing the block of code. The block of code under entry controlled loop does not get executed if the condition is false in the beginning.

Answer 2 :

(a)   false   (b) false   (c) true   (d) false   (e) false

Answer 3 :

(a) Error corrected   :   for (k = 0; k<10; k++)

(b) Error corrected   :   for (int m = 5; m > 1; m - -)

(c) Error corrected   :   for (int g = 1; g<= 5; g++)

(d) No Error

(e) Error corrected   :   for (c = 15; c < 20; c++)

Answer 4 :

(a) No output – as the condition is false in entry controlled loop. The loop is not getting executed at all.

(b) 4 5 6 7 8

(c) 15

(d) 25

CHAPTER 7 : NESTED FOR LOOPS

Answers 1 :

(a)
```
public class NestedLoop
{
    void main()
    {
        for (int r = 7; r >=1 ; r- - )
        {
            for(int c = 1; c <= r; c++)
            {
                System.out.print("   " + c);
            }
            System.out.println ( );
        }
    }
}
```

```
1 2 3 4 5 6 7
1 2 3 4 5 6
1 2 3 4 5
1 2 3 4
1 2 3
1 2
1
```

(b)
```
public class NestedLoop
{
    void main()
    {
        for (int r = 1; r <= 7; r++ )
        {
            for(int c = 1; c <= r; c++)
            {
                System.out.print("   " + c) ;
            }
```

```
1
1 2
1 2 3
1 2 3 4
1 2 3 4 5
1 2 3 4 5 6
1 2 3 4 5 6 7
```

```
                System.out.println ( ) ;
            }
        }
    }
```

(c)

```
    public class NestedLoop
    {
        void main()
        {
            for(int r = 1; r <= 5; r++)
            {
                for(int c=1; c<= r; c++)
                {
                    System.out.print(" ");
                }
                for(int d = r; d <= 7; d++)
                {
                    System.out.print(" " + d);
                }
                System.out.println ( );
            }
        }
    }
```

```
1  2  3  4  5  6  7
   2  3  4  5  6  7
      3  4  5  6  7
         4  5  6  7
            5  6  7
```

(d)

```
    public class NestedLoop
    {
        void main()
        {
            for(int r = 1; r <= 5; r++)
            {
                for(int c= 5; c >= r; c - - )
                {
                    System.out.print(" ");
                }
                for(int d = 1; d <= r; d++)
                {
                    System.out.print(" " + d);
                }
                System.out.println ( );
```

```
            1
         1  2
      1  2  3
   1  2  3  4
1  2  3  4  5
```

```
                }
            }
        }
```

(e) public class NestedLoop
     {
         void main()
         {
             for(int r = 9; r >=5; r - -)
             {
                 for(int c=5; c <= r; c + +)
                 {
                     System.out.print(" ");
                 }
                 for(int d = r; d <= 9; d++)
                 {
                     System.out.print(" " + d);
                 }
                 System.out.println ( ) ;
             }
         }
     }

```
            9
          8 9
        7 8 9
      6 7 8 9
    5 6 7 8 9
```

Answer 2.

(a) void main()
     {
         for (r = 1; r <= 5; r++)
         {
             for(c = r ; c >= 1; c - -)
             {
                 System.out.println ("   " + c) ;
             }
             System.out.print ( ) ;
         }
     }

(b) void main()
     {
         for (r = 50; r >= 25; r = r - 5)
         {
             for(c = 1; c <= 6; c++)
             {
                 System.out.print ("   " + r) ;
             }
             System.out.println ( ) ;
         }
     }

Answer 3.

(a)
```java
public class NestedLoop
{
      void main()
      {
            for(int r = 1 ; r <= 6; r + +)
            {
                  for(int c = 5 ; c <= 9; c++)
                  {
                        System.out.print(" # " + c + " * ") ;
                  }
                  System.out.println ( ) ;
            }
      }
}
```

(b)
```java
class Star
{
      void main()
      {
            int i, j;
            for( i =5; i >= 1; i --)
            {
                  for(j=1 ; j<= i  ; j++)
                  {
                        System.out.print("*");
                  }
                  System.out.println();
            }
      }
}
```

(c)
```java
public class NestedLoop
{
      void main()
      {
            int r = 0, c = 0;
            for ( r = 1 ; r<= 5; r ++ )
            {
                  for( c = r; c<= 5; c++)
                  {
                        System.out.print(" # ") ;
                  }
                  System.out.println( ) ;
            }
      }
}
```

```
(d)  class Pattern
     {
          void main ( )
          {
               Scanner sc = new Scanner(System.in);
               System.out.println("How many rows you want in this pattern?");
               int rows = sc.nextInt();
               System.out.println("Here is your pattern....!!!");
               for (int i = 7; i >= 1; i--)
               {
                    for (int j = 1; j <= i; j- -)
                    {
                         System.out.print( j + " " ) ;
                    }
                    System.out.println();
               }
          }
     }
```

CHAPTER 8 : COMPUTING AND ETHICS

Answer 1 : (a) Intellectual property   (b) Piracy   (c) netiquettes
       (d) Memory space   (e) Copyright   (f) Phishing
       (g) Hackers   (h) Authentication

Answer 2 : (a) [ii]   (b) [i]   (c) [iii]   (d) [iv]   (e) [iv]

Answer 3 : (a) Copyright   (b) trade secrets
       (c) patent   (d) virus

Answer 4 :

(a) Privacy is a fundamental human right recognized by the United Nations. A person decides how much of his private life and thoughts he wants to reveal and share.

Invading a person's privacy is a social crime and so it needs protection.

(b) Data protection means to safeguard your data when carrying out online transactions.

The Data Protection Act (DPA) protects the privacy and integrity of data held on individuals by businesses and other organizations. Only authorized people can change/update data of individuals. No objectionable data/comment should be present for individuals.

(c) Spams are unwanted e-mails sent from unknown people. These are bulk e-mails that are sent to people generally for advertising, phishing etc.

Viruses are harmful computer programs that cause damage to the information stored in the computer memory. They can hide themselves but can be felt when the computer shows unpredictable erroneous behaviour.

(d) **Authentication** is the process of protecting important and confidential data on the computer system using login ID and password.

Authorization refers to the process of protecting inappropriate access to resources on the computer system

Accounting refers to the tracking of network resources for the purpose of analysis, allocation and review. Tracking can be based on recording events such as the number of times an invalid password is entered by the user.

Confidentiality refers to the protection of information from access by unauthorized users.

(e) Two good rules of Email Etiquettes are :

* help new users

* use bcc in case a mail has to be sent/forwarded to various people

Two forbidden rules of Email Etiquettes

- ask other's email password
- open/read other's email account

www.ingramcontent.com/pod-product-compliance
Lightning Source LLC
LaVergne TN
LVHW080055160726
843469LV00047B/1820